Whispered Silences

Essay by Gary Y. Okihiro

Photographs by Joan Myers

A Samuel and Althea Stroum Book

University of Washington Press Seattle and London

Whispered Silences

Japanese Americans and World War II

This book

is published

with the

assistance of

a grant from

the Stroum

Book Fund,

established

through the

generosity of

Samuel and

Althea Stroum.

Copyright©1996 by the

University of Washington Press

Printed in Singapore

Design by Richard Hendel

Library of Congress Cataloging-in-Publication Data

Okihiro, Gary Y., 1945–

Whispered silences : Japanese Americans and World War II / essay by Gary Y. Okihiro ; photographs by Joan Myers.

p.   cm.

"A Samuel & Althea Stroum book."

Includes bibliographical references.

ISBN 0-295-97497-4 (cloth : alk. paper). —

ISBN 0-295-97498-2 (paper : alk. paper)

1. Japanese Americans—Evacuation and relocation, 1942–1945.

2. World War, 1939–1945—Concentration camps—United States.

3. World War, 1939–1945—Personal narratives, Japanese American.

I. Myers, Joan, 1944– . II. Title.

D769.8.A6O36   1996

940.53′1503956073—dc20   95-21895

CIP

TO SEAN AND COLIN

Contents

Author's Note Gary Y. Okihiro

During the fall of 1992, I received a letter from Joan Myers informing me that she was "looking for an author to do the text for a projected book." Myers explained that she was a fine-arts photographer with an interest in the relationship between people and the land. For the past four years she had been engaged in completing a series of photographs on all ten of the Japanese American concentration camps of World War II and was now seeking an author who, she proposed, could write "a text that is personal and alive with the daily activities, hopes, and tragedies of those who were incarcerated." Would I be interested in joining her in this project? she asked. "Our memories of history are short and ill informed in this country," Myers reminded me. "Prejudice and intolerance . . . have certainly not diminished since the 1940s. We need to be reminded that what happened to those of Japanese ancestry in the 1940s can happen again. None of us are free if we forget this dark moment of American history."

I was immediately tempted by this unexpected invitation, but the prospect of writing an extended essay on a subject I had written on before—although, to be sure, this time for the wider, lay audience envisioned by Myers—was a daunting challenge. My historical training and inclination tilts me toward careful, original research and a circumspect (turgid?) text, although my critics will likely disagree with that self-characterization. In addition, Myers asked that I put myself into the narrative to enable the readers to ascertain my location vis-à-vis my subject and to enliven the text with personality and passion. Of course, we understand that historical texts are revealing of both their authors and their subjects, but I felt uncomfortable about the thin line that separates (if indeed it separates) self-inscription from narcissism.

At first, I thought I would do what I ask my students to undertake: an essay on how Asian American history connects with their lives. I thought I would simply show how the wartime experience related to my life and that of my family. Now, having completed the project, I realize that my layered text attempts to make that link between past and present, social relations and individual agency, others and self, but it also uncovers a deeper stratum in my excavation of self and history. I employ personal memories and feelings to frame and speculate about the past, about what could have been, and thereby offer a parallel and complementary text to the oral histories and reminiscences I have assembled of those who experienced the central event of my narrative. Interwoven in my text, thus, are strands and fragments of personal memory, history, and the accounts of historical actors—a mixture that purposefully explores the borders and interstices of subject and object, subjectivity and objectivity.

Indeed, both Myers's photographs and my essay are personal readings of a historical event—the removal and detention of Japanese Americans during World War II—and as such constitute distinctive texts that are subject to multiple readings. Myers's photographs, accordingly, do not illustrate my narrative, and conversely, my words do not comment upon Myers's art. With separate eyes and from different directions, we have converged upon a space and time. Myers describes her sojourn in this place in the section that follows; I herewith explain mine.

This subject of Japanese Americans and World War II is clearly the most written-about episode in Asian American history and perhaps is the most recognized historical event of significance to Asian Americans among contemporary Americans. That memory is perpetuated, in both books and the public discourse, in large part by those who, like Myers, highlight the past to secure the future. For example, the Presidential Commission on Wartime Relocation and Internment of Civilians, created in 1980, recommended that funds be set aside for research and public education on the Japanese American detention and similar events, because, the commission wrote, "a nation which wishes to remain just to its citizens must not forget its lapses."

In truth, because of that focus upon the Japanese American wartime experience, I initially resisted Myers's kind invitation to me to join her in this project. I thought that other Asian American groups and other historical events and times demanded my attention. I thus was, at first, a reluctant partner. As I began to conceptualize the project and write, however, I became increasingly excited about my venture into what was for me uncharted territory, and am now exceedingly grateful to Myers for offering me this opportunity.

Assuredly, those who are already familiar with the subject matter will find that my historical narrative goes over well-trod terrain. But I think the landscape is decidedly mine. Although I have recorded the voices of many historical actors in my text, I have also selected and contextualized them. And I see the wartime experience not in isolation but in a progression of initiatives and interactions among and between Japanese Americans and others. My discussion of World War II, thus, is prefaced by a rather extended treatment of migration and settlement before the war and is followed by a reflection on the return and resettlement after the war. In addition, I try to view the times through the eyes of Japanese Americans and not of those who sought to shape and restrict their vision. Most writers recall the prewar period as a time when White politicians, patriots, labor leaders, and farmers fanned the flames of anti-Japanese hatred that culminated in the wartime detention. Instead, I attempt to understand how Japanese Americans experienced and negotiated those currents. Finally, I see links and parallels between Japanese Americans in Hawaii and on the mainland and accordingly move easily from one shore to the other, without, I hope, conflating two similar but also unique experiences.

I must acknowledge and thank my colleague in this venture, Joan Myers, for her cheerful persistence and patience in guiding me toward a new apprehension of myself and my work. Lane R. Hirabayashi, Roger Daniels, and Michael Kammen offered close readings of the text and helped to clarify and correct my account. I now understand more fully the simultaneous, mutual, and contested relationships I maintain with my texts and the contexts that condition my readings and renderings. But I also believe that I do not write for myself alone and acknowledge that I bear a special responsibility to the subjects and readers of my work, in whose debt and scrutiny I stand.

Parents mustn't miss a chance to rap with their children—our future—and it is to you, Sean and Colin, that I whisper these silences of our past.

Photographer's Note Joan Myers

T his work began in 1981, when I was on a family vacation and drove north from Los Angeles, through the Mojave Desert and along the eastern flank of the snow-covered Sierras. Two pagoda-roofed buildings caught my eye, and I pulled off the busy highway. In a parking area I read a small historical plaque identifying the site as the Japanese relocation center of Manzanar. Curious, I peered into the small stone buildings that I learned were entry stations for the camp. Then, for an hour or so, I walked in the chilly December wind treading my way carefully through the debris littering the grounds of the camp.

In the months that followed, I often recalled that walk. When the opportunity arose to visit southern California a year later, I returned to Manzanar, this time with my 4 × 5 view camera. I explored. Scratched into buckled ribbons of sidewalks I found the Japanese names of the internees who had mixed and poured the concrete. Nearby were crumbling barracks steps, low stone walls, the footings for guard towers, and a cemetery, each grave outlined with round stones and marked by a Japanese name. Empty ponds and extensive rock work from abandoned gardens lay partially obscured by dirt and fallen branches. Here in the Owens Valley, sucked dry in the 1920s by a thirsty Los Angeles, I could not tell if the trees that I saw, planted by camp internees, were still alive or merely skeletons standing desultory watch over the sites of the former barracks and gardens. Beyond the cement rubble, the rutted camp roads, and the parched bareness of the Owens Valley floor rose Mount Williamson and the sheer snow-covered eastern slope of the Sierras.

I wandered for several hours, taking it in, trying to understand, and, occasionally, taking a photograph. Although no barracks buildings remained, the ground was littered with small bits of construction debris and household trash: nails, scraps of pine lumber, tin cans, glass and china shards. Once, as I looked down to place the legs of my tripod, I noticed a piece of gray rubber half buried in sand. I reached down, pulled it carefully from its decades-old resting place, brushed off the dirt, and stared at a 1940s-vintage toy car, the rubber cracked from long exposure to the

13

elements. Who pushed this palm-sized car around in the sand fifty years ago? Did that child behind barbed wire remember a time when he rode in a real car with a favorite uncle to a family dinner? At that moment I resolved to learn and to share the stories of those who had to live in this barren place.

At home I began to read about the camps. In the panic after the bombing of Pearl Harbor in December of 1941, leaders in the Japanese American communities of the western United States were rounded up and sent to "internment camps," prisons run by the Justice Department. Within three months, everyone else of Japanese ancestry who remained on the West Coast was sent first to an assembly center and then to a camp administered by a new civilian agency, the War Relocation Authority. There were ten "relocation camps." In them, more than 110,000 people of Japanese ancestry, two-thirds of them American citizens, were interned for three years. No attempt was made to identify the potential threat to national security of an eighty-year-old grandmother, a ten-year-old orphan, a pregnant mother, or an immigrant shopkeeper or gardener. All left behind their friends, homes, and possessions for an undeclared period of time and an indefinite future.

When I researched the locations of the nine other relocation camps, I found them in some of the most desolate areas of the West: Poston in Arizona along the Colorado River, Gila River in central Arizona, Minidoka in Idaho, Amache in Colorado, Heart Mountain in Wyoming, Tule Lake in northern California, and Topaz in the salt flats of Utah. Jerome and Rohwer were in the swampy delta of the Mississippi River in Arkansas.

As I read, I planned trips to the remaining camps. When I went I found them in isolated locations and subject to extremes of temperature. Heart Mountain had strong winds and temperatures well below zero much of the winter. Gila River and Poston both reached over 100 degrees much of the summer. All of the camps had poisonous snakes: in the West, mainly rattlers; in Arkansas, four kinds of poisonous snake were in the high grasses. In all the camps the barracks in which the internees had lived had been removed after the war. Often they were sold to returning GIs, who moved them and used them as inexpensive, temporary housing. In some cases the land was sold and farmed or was used for low-cost housing projects, and most of the rubble was buried or hauled away. Everywhere some trace remains: a sewage treatment plant at Jerome, Arkansas; the cemetery at Rohwer, Arkansas; a school-house built by internees at Poston, Arizona.

Amache, in southeastern Colorado, was just a few miles from the route of the old Santa Fe Trail, where I was concluding a photographic project. Less dramatic in its setting than Manzanar, Amache was dark and full of stories. Many of the foundations for barracks still lay below the partial shade of dying cottonwood trees planted as saplings by internees fifty years before. With a map I could see where the administration buildings had been, the post office, a baseball field. Back home, I continued reading. So many stories. Thousands of lives and hopes. Small towns behind barbed wire with vegetable and flower gardens, flag raisings, Girl Scout meetings, dances, school classes, births, and deaths.

Often as I photographed, local farmers or ranchers stopped to find out what I was doing with my strange-looking camera and dark cloth. At Poston, while I was photographing the school building, a couple drove up, got out, and introduced themselves. Mr. Sato told me that he and his wife met "at camp." His barracks, he said, was about three-fourths of the way between the school and the haystack to which he pointed in a field. His wife, a gray-haired delicate woman in her sixties, lived in another section of the camp. They met at the Colorado River, about a four-mile hike for each of them, and gradually fell in love. The heat had been terrible, she said, 120 degrees in the summer. He told me he brought back carp from the river to put in the fish garden his family built outside their barracks. They stood close together quietly for a moment, and then Mr. Sato said, "We came back to see it after forty years."

It took me four years (1982–85) to reach all the camps and to photograph them. Though the process has been slow, I have wanted the work to be publicly available. My grandfather, Henry A. Wallace, was vice president in the second Roosevelt administration, in the early forties. Although he had no direct responsibility for the decision to deprive Japanese Americans of their civil rights, I feel in a small way personally accountable. The stories hidden in the concrete remains of the camps and told so movingly by historian Gary Okihiro must be heard. Unless those stories are heard, the unjust detention of all Japanese Americans during World War II could happen to another group of Americans at any time.

I am thankful for the encouragement and assistance of many people over the years, most particularly Gary DeWalt, who always believed in the work. He accompanied me to several of the camps, swatted mosquitoes at Topaz, nearly stepped on a snake at Gila River, and drove calmly through a ferocious dust storm en route to Minidoka, Idaho.

Many people were helpful at specific camps. I would like to especially thank Les and Nora Bovee at Heart Mountain, Wyoming, Jane Beckwith at Topaz, Utah, June Freeman and Mr. and Mrs. Sam Yada in Arkansas, Kenneth Hubbell of the Arkansas Endowment for the Humanities, and Virginia Ricketts in Twin Falls, Idaho. Nancy Araki from the Japanese American National Museum was interested and encouraging over many years.

A special thanks is due those who showed the work early on: Linda Durham in Santa Fe, the Center for Creative Photography in Tucson, and Marcuse Pfeifer in New York. Also, I am grateful to the National Endowment for the Arts in Arizona, which funded a multimedia collaborative presentation on the camps with poet Lawson Inada, composer Greg Steinke, and myself.

Although Gary Okihiro and I never met before the book was submitted for publication, I came to greatly admire his integrity and professionalism through our several-year correspondence. I am grateful for his willingness to fit a text to an already existing body of photographs and to bare his own past in the writing.

This book accompanies a Smithsonian Institution Traveling Exhibition Service (SITES) exhibit entitled *Whispered Silences: Japanese American Detention Camps, Fifty Years Later.* Though the book and the exhibition were conceived and produced independently, it is to the credit of all involved that they were finished on similar deadlines. I would like to acknowledge the SITES staff, especially Jennifer Thissen, Jim Rubenstein, and Betsy Hennings, who produced and arranged the touring show.

In the publication process, I feel fortunate to have had splendid support. Beth Hadas was very helpful in the preliminary stages of the publication process. Naomi Pascal, editor-in-chief at the University of Washington Press, enthusiastically accepted the book for publication. I am grateful to her, to designer Richard Hendel, to my exacting and encouraging editor, Pamela J. Bruton, to Veronica Seyd and others at the Press for their goodwill, attention to detail, and determination to produce a fine book.

Finally, an armful of golden sunflowers for my assistant, Sarah Hasted, who not only helped print the images for book reproduction but also brought good humor and calm enthusiasm to a lengthy and occasionally stressful process.

Whispered Silences

Entry station, Manzanar, California

View from memorial built by internees in 1944, Gila River, Arizona

Camp road, Amache, Colorado

Bath and latrine building foundation, Amache, Colorado

Sewage treatment plant, Jerome, Arkansas

Foundation with garden stone, Amache, Colorado

Hospital foundation, Heart Mountain, Wyoming

Medicine bottle

Homemade sign

Hospital debris, Heart Mountain, Wyoming

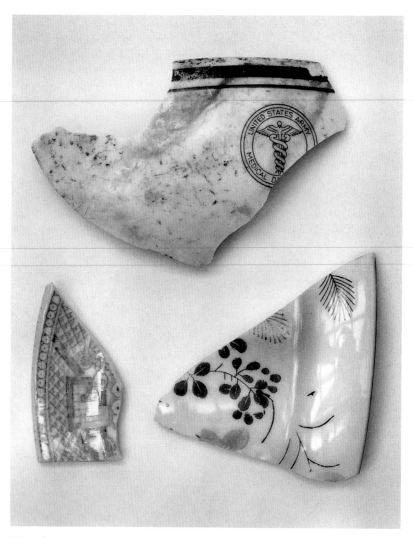

China shards

Hospital boiler house, Amache, Colorado

Metal objects

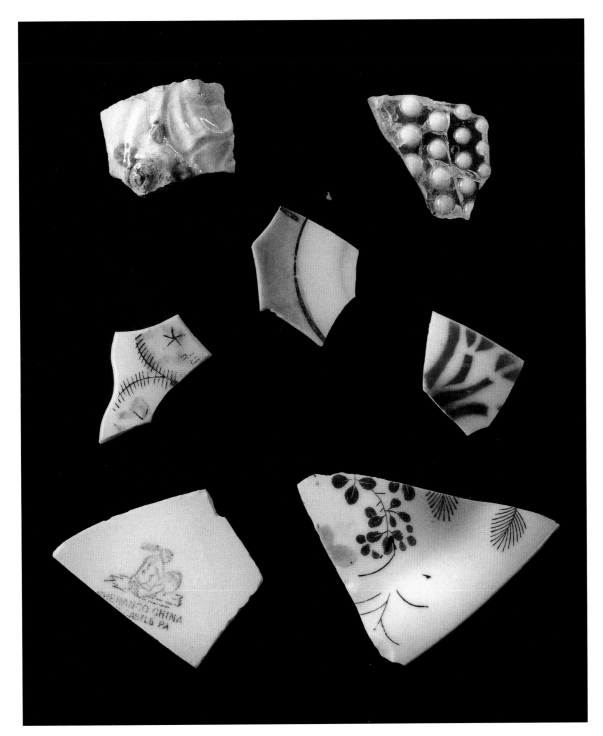

China shards

Tin patches used to cover knotholes in barracks

Remaining barracks building, Poston, Arizona

Potato cellar vents, Heart Mountain, Wyoming

Interior of potato cellar, Minidoka, Idaho

Stovepipes, Topaz, Utah

Caucasian housing, Heart Mountain, Wyoming

China dump, Manzanar, California

Spoon and china

Cola bottle

Mount Shasta, Tule Lake, California

Swimming pool diving board, Heart Mountain, Wyoming

Baseball backdrop, Topaz, Utah

Hinge

File

Paintbrush

War Department license plate

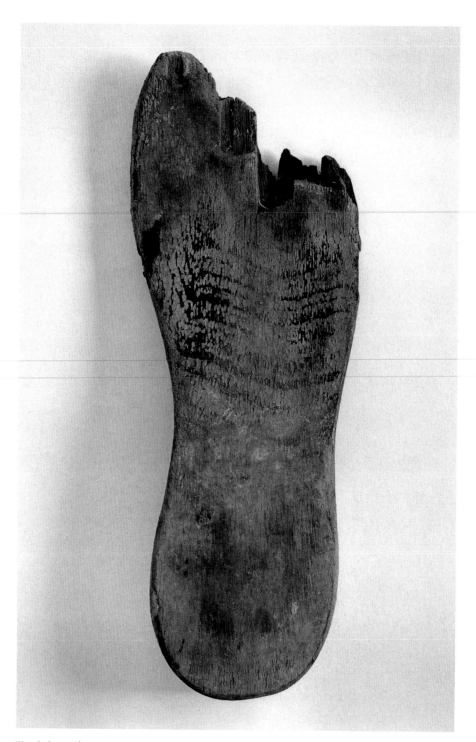

Wood shoe sole

Army boot

Silverware

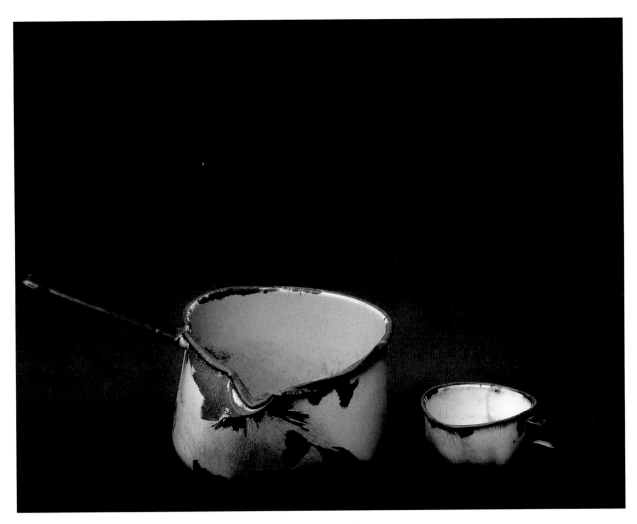

Pan and cup

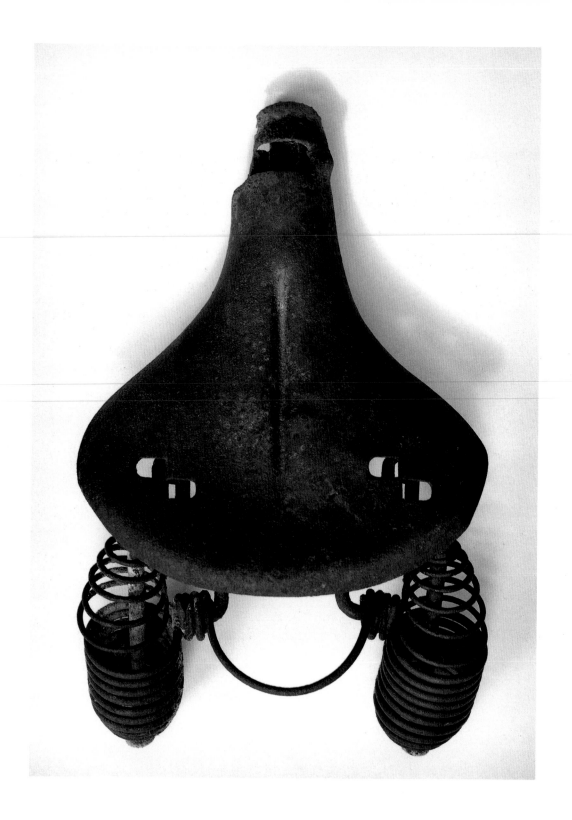

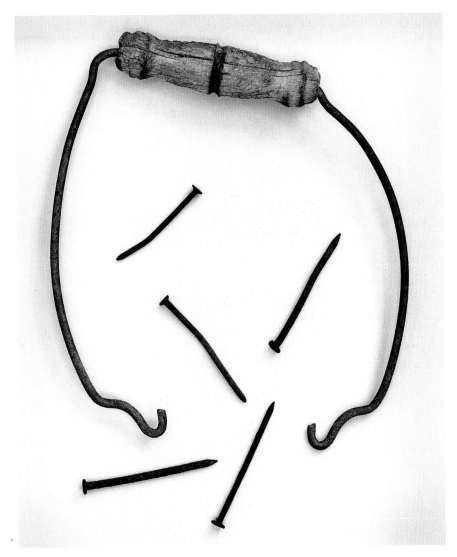

Pail handle and nails

Bicycle seat

Doorknob

School building plaque, Poston, Arizona

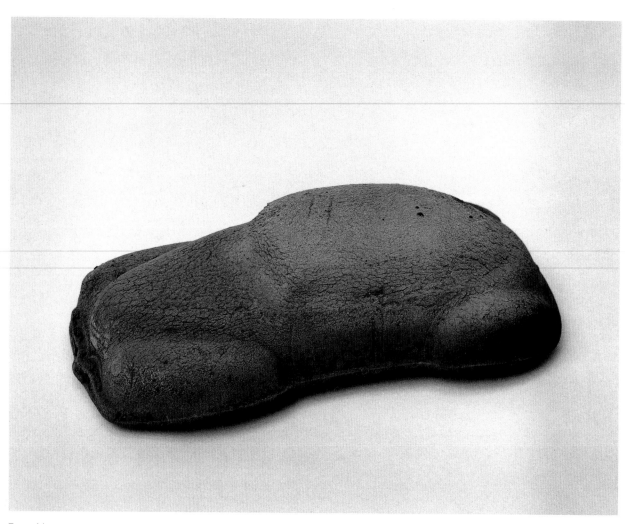

Toy rubber car

Girl Scout troop drawing

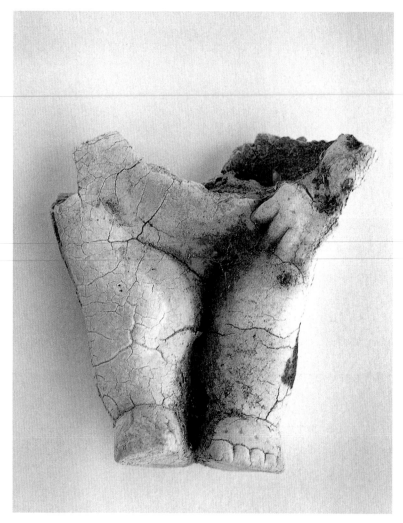

Toy rubber doll

Pet grave, Rohwer, Arkansas

Inscription, Gila River, Arizona

Inscription, Gila River, Arizona

Power plant smokestack, Jerome, Arkansas

Sewer cover, Topaz, Utah

Flyswatter

Garden for Caucasian housing, Manzanar, California

Garden, Manzanar, California

Garden, Manzanar, California

Garden, Manzanar, California

Bamboo garden, Manzanar, California

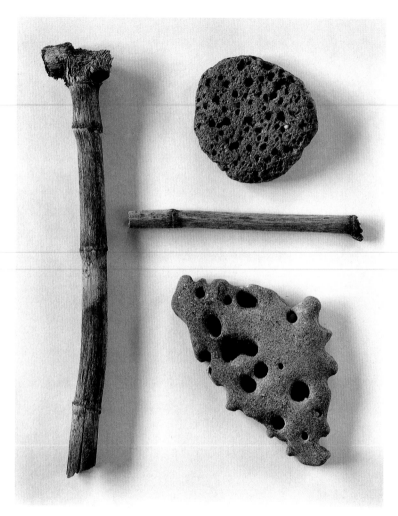

Garden objects

Garden, Gila River, Arizona

Victory garden, Topaz, Utah

Garden objects, Topaz, Utah

Wheelbarrow, Topaz, Utah

Cactus garden, Gila River, Arizona

Season's Greetings

Christmas card

Memorial to camp soldiers fighting in World War II, Gila River, Arizona

Steps leading to war memorial built by internees, Heart Mountain, Wyoming

Tombstone of sixty-year-old man who died June 27, 1944, Amache, Colorado

War Relocation Authority badge

Entrance guard station, Minidoka, Idaho

Guard tower footings, Manzanar, California

Cold

Cold. The wind was bitterly cold. As I crawled out of the weather-beaten, red Volkswagen bug, I pulled my jacket tightly around me and braced myself against the swirling wind. All around was desolation. My traveling companions joined me as I explored the remains of what had been a bustling town of 10,046 women, men, and children at its peak in November 1945. This was Manzanar, or "apple orchard," so named by eighteenth-century Spanish invaders of the valley.

I was on a quest, a pilgrimage. The year was 1972, and I was a graduate student at the University of California, Los Angeles. I had just returned after three years in Botswana, the antipode of my birthplace, Hawaii. There I had met and married Elizabeth Ritch, of Scotland and the Orkney isles, we two island lovers in a land-locked, desert nation. I had returned to UCLA to resume my graduate studies in African history, when I was caught up in the fervor of the times. Liberation, self-determination, equality, justice, those were our insistent demands, for full inclusion within the promise of America.

But where were our stories within the master narrative of American history? And how were they told, from whose perspective? I remember how the silences of the past were deafening to us. I remember how the strident and subtle distortions filled us with rage. I remember how history's whispers sent us scurrying, searching for our identity, as Asians, as Americans, as Asian Americans. We caught snippets of hushed conversation among our parents and elders, and we knew that our lives were firmly fixed within this land, but we didn't know how deep or how extensive were those roots. I was determined to unearth my buried past.

Located some 200 miles northeast of Los Angeles, Manzanar was one of those key burial sites, made sacred by the littered remains of my ancestors. I shivered in the morning cold. Somber gray mountains thrust upward by powerful tectonic forces rose from the valley floor to the west. That massive fracture in the earth's crust, forming the Sierra Nevada, could be traced from the tip of South America, up through Mexico and California, bending in an arc across Canada and Alaska, and down through the islands of Japan and the Philippines, constituting the "ring of fire" that borders the Pacific basin. Looking westward from Manzanar, the high, cold Sierras might have reminded one of the mountains of Japan, to which they were ultimately connected, but they also formed a granite curtain that sealed off the valley from the freedom of the boundless sea.

The Sierras, topped by Mount Whitney at their highest point, dominated the visual and emotional landscape. One always felt the mountains' presence. But the high-desert sand, the flat and featureless plain that stretched out from one's feet to the horizon north and south, was also a part of the reality that impinged constantly upon one's spatial sensibility. When photographer Ansel Adams brought his cameras to Manzanar in the fall of 1943, he observed: "I believe that the arid splendor of the desert, ringed with towering mountains, has strengthened the spirit of the people of Manzanar. I do not say all are conscious of this influence, but I am sure most have responded, in one way or another, to the resonances of their environment."[1]

The place was indeed sacred. I felt it within my bones, as I wandered through the remains of the camp. I easily made out the concrete foundations and support blocks, and determined which ones served as barracks for the internees and which ones as the toilets, washrooms, and mess halls. I could see them, as clearly as the desert sky, the flimsy structures of two-by-fours covered with tar paper nailed to joists with wood strips. Small windows let light into barren rooms barely ten by twenty feet, but they also let in the cold and heat and the ever present dust and sand. Row upon row of those barracks, spare and drab, extended in straight lines that converged where the earth met the sky.

Voices still echoed in that empty desert place, the waves washing across Owens Valley from the Sierras in the west to the Inyo and White Mountains in the east. The voices of Manzanar's children could be heard still, in the mute toys they left behind—a rusty car, a doll's head, a tricycle seat—still there, long after the wind had obliterated their companions' tiny footprints in the mud and sand. And because of the lucid stillness, I distinctly heard Manzanar's women and men in the broken china and bent forks heaped at the garbage dump, in the stone paths that led to their living quarters, in the ruin that was once a magnificent reflecting pool. Although bound to the earth, the pool's waters had mirrored the freedom of the skies. I thought I heard those voices in the morning chill.

"The sun was going down as we started along the muddy track, and a cold

1. John Armor and Peter Wright, *Manzanar* (New York: Times Books, 1988), p. xvii.

piercing wind swept in from the bay," remembered writer Yoshiko Uchida of 1942 and her first day at Tanforan Assembly Center just south of San Francisco. "When we arrived, there were six long weaving lines of people waiting to get into the mess hall. We took our place at the end of one of them, each of us clutching a plate and silverware borrowed from friends. . . . Shivering in the cold, we pressed together trying to shield Mama from the wind. As we stood in what seemed a breadline for the destitute, I felt degraded, humiliated, and overwhelmed with a longing for home. And I saw the unutterable sadness on my mother's face."[2]

"The sky turned steel grey," wrote artist Estelle Ishigo of the winter of 1942 in Heart Mountain concentration camp in Wyoming. "Icy winds blew long white drifts of clouds over the roofs. Our clothes were becoming far too thin. Shabby, shivering people stood in line for G.I. socks, underwear, coats and wool pants. . . . We looked beyond the mountain into the cold, threatening sky and gazed with longing at the distant horizon—this country, our home, our refuge, our sanctuary now seemed far away."[3]

At Hawaii's Sand Island concentration camp in Honolulu harbor, Yasutaro Soga recalled how guards discovered a knife on Ryoshin Okano, a priest, on December 14, 1941, and how they strip-searched Okano and all of his work companions. Despite nightfall, wrote Soga, "we were gathered in the open space and we took off our clothes. We had to remain standing for a long time until they finished searching our clothes. Other guards searched our tents and took away our fountainpens and pencils. We were frozen to death in the cold, windy, and barren field."[4]

Cold. I cannot remember being colder than I was when I was in another desert far away from Manzanar, on another continent. The sun had already set when we clambered on top of the goods piled in the back of a lorry in Botswana, southern Africa. We were trying to get from Francistown to Maun toward the far west, deep in the heart of the Kalahari Desert. This was the only means of transportation we could find. About twenty of us had paid a modest sum for the ride, and we tried to hollow out a seat on the canvas that covered the cargo. I twisted my arm around one of the ropes that held the tarpaulin down to avoid being tossed off the truck as it sped into the night, hitting numerous bumps and potholes along the way. As the minutes became hours, I felt the full blast of the cold night air, and I lost all sensation in my

2. Yoshiko Uchida, *Desert Exile: The Uprooting of a Japanese-American Family* (Seattle: University of Washington Press, 1982), pp. 70–71.
3. Estelle Ishigo, *Lone Heart Mountain* (Los Angeles: n.p., 1972), pp. 33–34.
4. Gary Y. Okihiro, *Cane Fires: The Anti-Japanese Movement in Hawaii, 1865–1945* (Philadelphia: Temple University Press, 1991), p. 217.

arms and legs. But most curiously to me, days later, my teeth and jaws ached because I must have clamped down on them so tightly as I shivered in the cold.

But cold can numb the mind as well as the body, making one oblivious to the perceptions of the other senses—of sight and smell, hearing and taste. Growing up in Hawaii, I never thought of myself as a Japanese American. It never occurred to me. I thought of myself as a descendant of the Pilgrims, 1620 and all that. I, like my friends from Hawaii, China, Japan, Korea, the Philippines, Puerto Rico, the Azores, and Samoa, was told by Japanese and Chinese teachers that as Americans we shared a common ancestry that could be traced to Jamestown and Plymouth Rock. I read scores of books about our national heroes, about John Smith and William Bradford, John Winthrop and Roger Williams, Patrick Henry and the Sons of Liberty. I imagined myself going to grandma's house in a horse-drawn wagon, tapping maple syrup in the spring, and ice-skating on frozen Walden Pond. My everyday reality of equatorial sunshine, heat, and humidity, the sugar fields that bordered our plantation camp home, and our evening meals that always featured rice and vegetables grown in our backyard failed to tarnish my carefully nurtured New England pedigree.

Oh, I knew that I was Japanese American, alright. My mother's warning about my Chinese playmate, "be careful about what they eat," and our cruel teasing of the *haole* ("White") girl who wore leg braces to support her polio-wracked body and who lived in the house behind us told me who I was not. And my grandmother's Okinawan doughnuts and my grandfather's Japanese mutterings, my annual attendance at *bon odori* in the late summer commemorating the spirits of the dead, and my years of *karate* lessons told me who I was. But like so many of my generation, the *sansei* (third), I was shielded from the Japanese American past because of the lessons my parents and their generation, the *nisei* (second), learned from World War II: avoid things Japanese.

You see, things Japanese were un-American. Even before the war, America's Japanese had been admonished to "speak, dress, and think American," and during the days following Pearl Harbor, both in Hawaii and on the U.S. mainland, Japanese Americans buried Japanese flags, letters sent from their kinfolk in Japan, and Japanese-language books and records—indeed, all things Japanese. They constituted a veritable and literal buried past. My mother told me how my grandfather smashed her prized collection of Japanese records the day after Japan's attack. Any connection, any link with Japan, any expression, any thoughts indicative of Japanese culture and ethnicity, invited others' suspicion, he had told her. Japanese appearances, words, and deeds had to be hidden within the confines of the home, and even that haven was spied upon by vigilant children who fingered their parents and grandparents. Born about two months after Japan's surrender, I was given a Japanese name—Yukio—but this was placed between my English first name and my family name as if to hide my true identity and protect me from anti-Japanese stares.

My Japanese American past, thus, was buried by the shapers of the national identity and my parents and me insofar as we had bought into the notion of my New England genealogy and adopted the counsel to "speak, dress, and think American." But like the immigrant Jewish mother in the film *Hester Street* who secretly put salt in the pocket of her child as he was about to venture out for the first time into the American world, our parents whispered in our ears as they put grains of rice in our pockets to protect us from the dangers of the unknown and to remind us of our true origins.

Hanayo Inouye, bound for America in the early 1900s, recalled leaving her mother at the Hiroshima train station. " 'I am going to miss you very much when you leave,' " her mother told her, " 'but I'll always be with you. We won't be separated even for a moment.' At first I did not know what she was talking about," admitted Inouye. "Later that night when I was undressing myself to go to sleep, I understood what she meant. I found a piece of the Buddhist altar ornament in the breast of my kimono. I was so sad when I left her at the station that I didn't know it was there. When I found it, I thought, 'She is with me after all, my mother.' " [5]

Packed in our trunks by our mothers like homemade underwear, in the memorable analogy of Asian American writer Maxine Hong Kingston, those grains, those ornaments, those undergarments, eventually steered us to the question of our ethnic identity. The past, of course, comprised the foundations of our homebase, of our claim to America, our sense of self and place.

We—Asian Americans—discovered our birthplace in California, but also in Hawaii, Washington, Texas, Louisiana, New York. We recognized it, and found it in the stories of our parents and grandparents, in their voices, in their language.

5. Eileen Sunada Sarasohn, ed., *The Issei: Portrait of a Pioneer* (Palo Alto: Pacific Books, 1983), p. 37.

Silenced for far too long, their stories poured forth and opened other channels; they "burst with telling" in the words of Japanese Canadian writer Joy Kogawa. Those stories were collected and shared, they were circulated like snapshots among family and friends, who colored them with their readings and slipped them into our community's family album, into our collective memory. And with remembrance came a gradual thawing of the numbness brought on by the cold and a return of some feeling and flexibility. Our minds could expand, our bodies stand erect. But the process moved in fits and starts. Healing takes time, we told ourselves.

At first, some of us sought authenticity in our Asian roots. Go to the source was our mantra. I shall never forget my first visit to Japan in 1970. I was on my way back to Hawaii from Africa after a two-year stint with the Peace Corps in Botswana. Volunteers who extended their tour of service as I did were encouraged to return home after their second year to reestablish the primordial ties with the homeland and thereby break the spell that the foreign host country held over them. The agency was quick to remind us that Peace Corps service in a faraway land was but a gig; our real lives awaited us at home in America. Asian migrants who went to America were similarly encouraged to remember their kinfolk in Asia by sending remittances that would buy food for the living and incense for the dead.

I landed in Osaka. I felt free. At last, I was "home." Everyone looked like me. This was the "motherland." I quickly unpacked and left my hotel on foot, wanting to mingle with "my people." The night air was crisp. Brightly colored neon signs were everywhere. I choked back tears of pride in my people, my kind who had created this marvel of technology from the ashes of war, and I walked and walked. I soon realized that I was lost, hopelessly lost. Because the streets were not parallel and I could not read, I failed to recognize markers and directions. Eventually I stumbled into a brightly lit street with seemingly endless rows of *pachinko* machines, each attended to by an engrossed player intently flipping the ball bearings through their courses. I wandered aimlessly through the maze happy in my secret communion with my brothers. A small group of women stood in the middle of the street, and as I strolled by, one of them approached me. "Do you want sex?" she whispered in my ear. Startled, I blurted out in English, "Why no. No, I'm not interested," and waved my hands as if to ward off her untoward advance. She examined my face skeptically, looking me over to see if I was indeed Japanese. "*Baka, bakatare* [stupid, stupid]," she yelled at me as I desperately sought the anonymity of the crowd. This was not my home, I told myself, after I showed the taxi driver my hotel's business card, written in Japanese.

Japanese American is not Japanese, I learned that night in Osaka. And like many of my generation, I soon realized that my ethnic identity had not been imported intact from the "motherland" but also bore the label "made in America." The search for my story's beginning, accordingly, shifted from Asia to America, and my focus centered on the first-generation immigrants. The arrival of the *issei*, or first generation, comprised the when and where of my beginning.

I discovered, much to my surprise, that the first Japanese migrants were as much driven by conditions in Japan as by recruiters who sought workers for the plantations and fields of Hawaii and the West Coast. Japanese came to America, but first Americans went to Japan to "open" Japan to American markets in 1853 and later to secure laborers for America's industries. "We are in much need of them," wrote Robert Crichton Wyllie, Hawaiian foreign minister and master of Princeville Plantation on the island of Kauai, to an American businessman in Japan in 1865. "Could any good agricultural laborers be obtained from Japan or its dependencies, to serve like the Chinese, under a contract for 6 or 8 years?" Eugene M. Van Reed, the businessman, wrote back to Charles de Varigny, Wyllie's successor: "No better class of people for Laborers could be found than the Japanese race, so accustomed to raising Sugar, Rice, and Cotton, nor one so easily governed, they being peaceable, quiet, and of a pleasant disposition."

On May 17, 1868, the *Scioto* slipped from its mooring in Yokohama and set sail for Honolulu, carrying on board 141 men, 6 women, and 2 children. Among the *gannenmono*, or "first-year people" (so named because they migrated during the first year of the Meiji era), were Tomisaburo Makino, an armorer to samurai and group spokesman; nineteen-year-old Tomi Ozawa, who was eight-months' pregnant, and her husband, Kintaro; a thirteen-year-old heavy drinker nicknamed "Ichi the Viper"; a few samurai, a hairdresser, cooks, potters, printers, *sake* brewers, tailors, and woodworkers. A stowaway, Yonekichi Sakuma, kept a diary of the voyage, giving us glimpses of life on board the ship. Peering through bags of rice and tubs of *shoyu* (soy sauce) and *miso* (fermented soybean paste), Sakuma noted that many of the passengers suffered from seasickness during the first few days. Later, he wrote, men whiled away the time polishing rice (rubbing the husks off the grain), engaging in horseplay, and stealing a smoke, the penalty for which involved the handcuffing of the smoker. Twelve days before sighting land, Kodzu Wakichi died and was buried at sea.

On June 19, 1868, the *Scioto* cast anchor in Honolulu harbor. The *gannenmono* were greeted with a gift of salted fish from the Hawaiian king and were given a two-week rest period to recuperate from the sea voyage. "They are a very good natured and lusty looking set of fellows," reported the June 24, 1868, *Hawaiian Gazette*. "They are favorably received by our population, both Hawaiian and foreign, and the impression is prevalent that they will make peaceable and efficient laborers, and give satisfaction." Sugar plantations on Maui, Oahu, Kauai, and Lanai paid $70 for each contract that bound a worker to three years of service for a monthly wage of $4 and food and lodging.

Within a month, planters and laborers lodged complaints with the Bureau of Immigration. M. McInerny asked for a refund and compensation for Nakasuke, a domestic servant who was constantly ill and required hospitalization. Theophilus H. Davies, agent for Kaalaea Plantation, wrote for a full refund for a *gannenmono* who died shortly after collapsing in the field. The incident, he explained, was "the occasion of much delay as he had to be tended by the men who were greatly needed at their own work." The Japanese workers protested against the planters' practice of withholding half of their wages each month, requested paid holidays, and challenged the transfer of their contracts from one plantation to another. The bureau ruled that planters could not withhold workers' monthly wages, but continued discontent led to the return of forty *gannenmono* before the completion of their contracts through an agreement between the governments of Japan and Hawaii. The returnees charged the planters with cruelty toward the workers and with reneging on the terms of their contracts.

Thirteen of the *gannenmono* returned to Japan after completing their three-year contracts, and the remainder applied to stay in Hawaii. A number of the men married Hawaiian women. Matsugoro Kuwada, a tailor on Maui, married Meleana

Auwekoolani; Bunkichi Arai married Lucy Kahalekai Hanapi of Kauai; Yonekichi Sakuma, the stowaway, married Papuka Kolia; Tokujio Sato, of Pahoa, Hawaii, married Kalala Kamekona; and Toyokichi Fukumura married Luka Kaha of Molokai. Their children added to the significant bicultural group of Hawaiian Asians and marked the beginning of a diverse Japanese community in Hawaii. Tomi Ozawa was the only woman from among the "first-year people" to remain in the islands; her son Yotaro became a policeman, her son Arthur became an attorney, and her daughter Itoko became a translator for Hawaii's minister to Japan.

The first Japanese settlement on the U.S. mainland was not the result of labor recruiters as in Hawaii but was an outcome of political conditions in Japan that were in part brought about by America's "opening" of the Tokugawa shogunate's closed doors. The Meiji Restoration that followed contact with the West ended 268 years of Tokugawa rule, and those who had supported the shogunate were stripped of their power and influence. One such feudal lord was Matsudaira Katamori, who had as one of his advisors John Henry Schnell (Hiramatsu Buhei), a European married to a Japanese woman. Schnell suggested to his lord that migration to America might afford him refuge and allow him to reestablish his feudal privileges. Katamori sent Schnell and an advance party of farmers, samurai, and four women to establish the Wakamatsu Tea and Silk Farm Colony, named after the lord's dominion, Aizu Wakamatsu.

Schnell, his wife, their two daughters, their servant Okei Ito, and the settlers arrived in San Francisco on May 27, 1869, on board the S.S. *China*. They brought with them tea seeds, grape seedlings, bamboo shoots, and thousands of mulberry trees for silk farming. Schnell purchased 600 acres near Placerville, California, for the farm colony, but the soil was dry, water for irrigation was scarce, and the plants soon withered and died. When financial support from Japan failed to come, Schnell left with his wife and children, promising to return with money, but he did not return.

Some of the settlers might have found their way back to Japan; others simply drifted off and became a part of the American West. The Schnell family servant, nineteen-year-old Okei Ito, died of a fever and was buried at the site of the failed colony on Gold Hill. Her gravestone, probably erected by Matsunosuke Sakurai and the remaining colonists, bore the inscription "In memory of Okei, died 1871, age 19 years, a Japanese girl." Sakurai, a samurai and carpenter for the colony, lived until about 1900 and was buried in Coloma, not far from Gold Hill. Another of the original colonists, Kuninosuke Masumizu, married an African American woman and ran a fish store in Sacramento for many years. The couple had three daughters and a son, George, who operated a barber shop in Sacramento. Together with the bicultural children of Hawaii's *gannenmono*, Masumizu's bicultural children were the beginning of Japanese America.

Students, political exiles, diplomats, contract laborers, prostitutes, men, women, and children soon followed the currents that had brought the earliest Japanese migrants to Hawaii and the U.S. mainland. But even before those first pioneers, as early as 1865, several hundred Japanese students attended Amherst College, Cornell, Harvard, Princeton, and Yale. In late-nineteenth-century California, Japanese "schoolboys" performed domestic service for White families while attending school during the day. Unaccustomed to European American households and to performing "women's work," young men learned to start fires, set the table, prepare meals, and clean windows and floors. "One of my friends endeavoured to make a fire by burning the kindling in the oven," recalled Yone Noguchi. "Another one was on the point of blowing out the gaslight. One fellow terrified the lady when he began to take off his shoes, and even his trousers, before scrubbing the floor. . . . I rushed into my Madam's toilet room without knocking. The American woman took it good-naturedly, as it happened."[6]

Some of the first migrant Japanese women, lured to the United States by con men flashing money and spinning tales of gold in America, were forced into lives of prostitution. "I'm a daughter of a farming household in Amakusa," said a prostitute. "Around 1889-90 a smooth-talking man appeared on my island." The man told fantastic stories of far-off places, like Southeast Asia, where children played with pearls and corals, and America, where gold nuggets lay on riverbanks waiting to be picked up. Intrigued by his stories, she accompanied him to the port of Nagasaki, where he took her on board a large steamship. Before she realized what was happening, the ship sailed off for San Francisco, where she was given a dress and taken off the ship by a sailor. "Pulled by his hand in the pitch darkness of the night, I just trailed be-

6. Yuji Ichioka, *The Issei: The World of the First Generation Japanese Immigrants, 1885–1924* (New York: Free Press, 1988), p. 25.

hind him. I arrived at an unknown house and was introduced to other women," she recalled, ending her account at that point.[7]

Japanese prostitutes worked with African, Chinese, Irish, and French prostitutes throughout the American West. "It was in August, 1902, when I came to America," recalled Bunshiro Tazuma. "To my surprise, I found at least two to six Japanese prostitutes in every town where I went between Seattle and St. Paul, a range of two thousand miles. Even when I went to Alaska . . . I was surprised to see from two to five or six in such towns as Ketchikan, Juneau, Wrangell, Sitka and Skagway." Tazuma learned from sailors that an agent in Nagasaki promised women high wages for working as domestics to White families, but in ports like Victoria, Vancouver, Bellingham, and Olympia, they were sold for several hundred dollars to "local bosses." "Oppressed by a boss," observed Tazuma sadly, "it is said they could do nothing but weep for four or five years."[8] In truth, some of the leaders of the early Japanese community made their fortunes from the labor and misery of prostitutes, prompting a prostitute to remark: "From the way I see them [people in general], they're all whores. Whores without human feelings. . . . And people at large, in apparent glee, respect male whores who have power."[9]

Reformers, both Japanese and White, established missions for Japanese prostitutes, offering them shelter and finding them legitimate employment. Waka Yamada, the noted feminist writer and critic, was once a prostitute in Seattle. Lured to America in 1902 by a man's tales of easy wealth, Yamada was forced into prostitution under the name of "Oyae of Arabia." The following year she managed to escape to San Francisco, only to be captured and thrust into a Chinatown brothel. She fled a second time and succeeded in returning to Japan, where she educated herself and became a leading advocate of women's causes. In 1938, she revisited Seattle to deliver a speech on women's rights. She was shouted down by members of the audience in Japanese Hall until she revealed her past: "I dare to say these things because I myself had a hard experience!" she declared, whereupon the jeering stopped.[10]

During the 1870s, the governments of Japan and Hawaii agreed to suspend Japanese labor migration to the islands largely because of the acrimony engendered by the experience of the *gannenmono*. But an 1881 state visit to Japan by Hawaii's King

7. Ibid., pp. 31–32.
8. Kazuo Ito, *Issei: A History of Japanese Immigrants in North America*, trans. Shinichiro Nakamura and Jean S. Gerard (Seattle: Japanese Community Service, 1973), pp. 769–71.
9. Yuji Ichioka, "Ameyuki-san: Japanese Prostitutes in Nineteenth-Century America," *Amerasia Journal* 4, no. 1 (1977): 17.
10. Ito, *Issei*, p. 775.

Kalakaua was followed by an allocation of $50,000 by the kingdom's legislature for the promotion of Japanese labor migration to the islands. "Hawaii holds out her loving hand and heart to Japan and desires that your people may come and cast in their lots with ours and repeople our Island home," wrote the Hawaiian special envoy to Japan's Emperor Meiji.[11] The labor recruiters distributed advertisements throughout Japan but concentrated their efforts in Hiroshima, Kumamoto, and Yamaguchi Prefectures, from whence came the largest number of migrants. More than 28,000 applicants signed up for the 943 slots on the first shipload of "government-contract migrants," or *kanyaku imin*.

"Many Japanese at that time went to Hawaii under contracts to work on sugar cane plantations," explained Riichi Satow. "For a commission, Japanese agents recruited young people as contract laborers throughout the rural areas of Japan. There were a number of people who came to Hawaii that way, usually with a three-year contract."[12] Robert Walker Irwin, Hawaiian consul general and special agent for immigration in Japan from 1884 to 1894, delivered about 29,000 Japanese to Hawaii's plantations. Receiving commissions and other fees for each man and woman he sent, Irwin apparently built a personal fortune from the recruitment trade. Japanese, too, profited. Joji Nakayama was brought to Hawaii by Irwin to serve as an intermediary between the workers and plantation managers. For his services, Nakayama received an initial salary of $100 per month, in contrast to the $15 monthly salary of a plantation laborer at the time, and eventually collected $6,000 per year plus bonuses. One of the songs sung by Japanese workers was

The laborers keep on coming
Overflowing these Islands
But it's only Inspector Nakayama
Who rakes in the profits.[13]

Between 1885 and 1894, about 29,000 Japanese made the crossing to Hawaii as government-contract migrants, followed by approximately 125,000 Japanese who went to Hawaii as "free migrants" from 1894 to 1908, when Japanese migration was drastically curtailed by the Gentlemen's Agreement, which halted the further migration of male laborers. Women made up a mere 9 percent of Hawaii's Japa-

11. Okihiro, *Cane Fires*, p. 24.
12. Sarasohn, *Issei*, p. 24.
13. Franklin S. Odo and Harry Minoru Urata, "Hole Hole Bushi: Songs of Hawaii's Japanese Immigrants," *Mana* (Hawaii ed.) 6, no. 1 (1981): 72.

nese in 1890, but increased to 22 percent in 1900, 31 percent in 1910, and 41 percent in 1920. Paralleling those developments in Hawaii, about 27,440 Japanese entered the U.S. mainland from 1891 to 1900, and 42,457 more migrated between 1901 and 1907, joined by about 38,000 laborers who migrated from Hawaii to the mainland. Women constituted only 4 percent of the mainland Japanese in 1900, rising to 13 percent in 1910, and 35 percent in 1920. Women's rapid increase between 1910 and 1920 was largely attributable to the "picture brides," who were permitted under the terms of the Gentlemen's Agreement, which allowed the passage of the wives of those already in America.

Between 1910 and 1940, thousands of Chinese migrants passed through the wooden barracks on Angel Island. Like the 1908 Gentlemen's Agreement, the 1882 Chinese Exclusion Act had barred Chinese workers from the golden shore. America did not welcome Asia's "wretched refuse" with open arms. Instead, on the island, surrounded by the chilly waters of the bay, the migrants were questioned by skeptical U.S. immigration officials, who sought to ensure that the law was not violated. The poems carved on the walls by the detainees conveyed their anguish.

> Imprisoned in the wooden building day after day,
> My freedom withheld; how can I bear to talk about it?
> I look to see who is happy but they only sit quietly.
> I am anxious and depressed and cannot fall asleep.
> The days are long and the bottle constantly empty;
>   my sad mood, even so, is not dispelled.
> Nights are long and the pillow cold; who can pity my loneliness?
> After experiencing such loneliness and sorrow,
> Why not just return home and learn to plow the fields?[14]

"I left home in 1916 and got here on the ninth of February in 1917," recalled Kamechiyo Takahashi. She was taken from the ship to the immigration station on Angel Island. "I had never seen such a prison-like place as Angel Island," Takahashi exclaimed. "There were threefold wire nets on the wall. There was a big wire net outside, a thick wire net in the middle, and a screen door inside. I wondered why I had to be kept in a prison after I'd arrived. . . . I regretted having come, and I won-

14. Him Mark Lai, Genny Lim, Judy Yung, *Island: Poetry and History of Chinese Immigrants on Angel Island, 1910–1940* (Seattle: University of Washington Press, 1980), p. 68.

dered what the place I was going to would be like." Much to her relief, the pictures that her husband had sent to her showing his home and business in San Francisco were not retouched. "Later I was relieved to see that the business was prosperous," she said.[15]

In Seattle, Japanese migrants were held by immigration officials in the Detention House. Mitsuko Yoneyama described her quarantine there and that of nineteen other picture brides. "We were confined in a barren room all together with people who had been put in before us. Bunk beds were lined up in the room. The windows had iron bars, and the place looked like a jail. . . . I was seized by an indescribable loneliness. A lady returning to the States was sent back to Japan for some reason, and I wished I too would be sent back. After lights-out at 9 P.M., I used to scrawl with my pen in my diary by the dim light coming through the barred window."[16] Kikuyo Murata, another picture bride, spoke of the bad food served at the Detention House and remembered how Sumi Onishi smuggled a banana into the House and gave it to her. "It was so delicious that I almost cried," recalled Murata.[17]

Many of the Japanese who arrived in Hawaii and the U.S. mainland after 1908 were the wives and children of men admitted before exclusion. "I was six years old when my father went to the United States," said Tokushiga Kizuka. "Eleven years later . . . my father summoned me to work. My father came to meet me when I landed in San Francisco. Other than a picture, I had no idea how my father looked, and I did not recognize him—it was like we were strangers."[18] Family reunification involved the meetings of strangers—brides with grooms—whose marriages were arranged by matchmakers in Japan through photographs of the men in America and women in Japan. "Most of the people on board were picture brides," recalled Rikae Inouye. "I came with my husband. When the boat anchored, one girl took out a picture from her komono sleeve and said to me, 'Mrs. Inouye, will you let me know if you see this face?' She was darling. Putting the picture back into her kimono sleeve, she went out to the deck. The men who had come to pick up their brides were there. It was like that. I felt they were bold."[19]

Sagami Shinozawa married her husband, Shunso, while she was in Japan and he was in Hawaii. Instead of marrying the man selected by her parents, a man of high

15. Sarasohn, *Issei*, pp. 52–53.
16. Ito, *Issei*, p. 46.
17. Ibid., p. 47.
18. Sarasohn, *Issei*, pp. 49–50.
19. Ibid., p. 51.

social status, Sagami convinced her parents to allow her to become Shunso's picture bride. The wedding ceremony, held at the home of the bride's parents, was preceded by a procession to her husband's home in the next village. Arriving at the home at dusk, she was greeted by her in-laws and relatives in the pathway with lighted lanterns. After returning home, she chose to exchange nuptial cups of *sake* with herself, facing Shunso's photograph, rather than having a proxy play the role of her groom. Sagami traveled to Hawaii, worked with her husband in the cane fields, and, after his death, remained in the islands and supported herself by working in the fields. Although she was ridiculed by her women coworkers for being too slow, she eventually became one of the first *issei* woman overseers at the Oahu Sugar Company.[20]

Reading those accounts, I thought about my grandmother, who arrived in Hawaii as a young picture bride. One summer's night, I sat with my mother and her mother and father in the house we called "up-house" in Aiea Plantation camp. The Kakazu family home was simply "up-house" because it stood next door to our house, just above us. My grandmother was on the porch, seated in her favorite rocking chair, watching the sun dip behind the Waianae range of mountains and looking nowhere in particular into the distance. That was her evening ritual. My mother and I joined her on the porch for a while until the mosquitoes drove us inside. There, my grandfather sat on his chair under the lamp reading his Japanese newspaper, pretending not to listen to our conversation as we settled next to my grandmother.

"I was born on September 17, 1898, in Osatomura, Okinawa," she began. "My mother, Kame Shiroma, and my father, Kame Chinen, were both farmers. I was the second born, with an older sister and a younger brother." She remembered having a rather pampered life as a child, her parents being relatively well-off, and never worked in the field while attending school. When she was about seventeen years old, her aunt came to her parents with an offer of marriage from Kashin Kakazu in Hawaii, a man about ten years her senior and known only to her aunt. My grandmother talked over the idea of marrying and moving to Hawaii with several of her schoolmates, who all thought what a splendid adventure and opportunity this would be. "You see," she explained, "my elder sister had married and gone to Kauai and had done well, and we knew of other girls who had gone. Hawaii seemed like a good

20. Barbara F. Kawakami, *Japanese Immigrant Clothing in Hawaii, 1885–1941* (Honolulu: University of Hawaii Press, 1993), pp. 22–24.

place." She accepted the proposal, and her parents, despite their misgivings about their second daughter leaving for Hawaii, gave their blessing to the marriage. Her name was recorded next to the name of Kashin Kakazu at the village temple; they were married.

Before leaving, she assured her parents that she would return after three years, and later, she felt betrayed by the promise of quick riches in Hawaii and the reality of stifling work and recurrent pregnancies that prevented her from seeing her parents again. On board the *Satora Maru*, she regretted her decision, missed her mother dearly, and was constantly seasick. She was miserable. Finally, she and her fellow passengers arrived at Honolulu harbor and were escorted to the old immigration station, where she remained for about three weeks. There she was subjected to physical examinations that were demeaning and daily questioning about her motives for coming to Hawaii. The problem, she explained, was that Grandfather had been married to another woman, whom he had divorced by simply sending her back to Okinawa to her parents. He did not have a legal, American divorce. The authorities, thus, suspected that she was either joining a bigamous husband or being brought into Hawaii to work as a prostitute. Of the nearly three dozen picture brides with whom she had arrived, my grandmother was the last to leave the immigration building.

My grandfather, his white hair glowing in the lamplight, put down his paper and chimed in: "Yes, I had a hard time convincing the immigration officer that I was a single man." Knowing something about my grandfather, I could not help thinking that he must have bribed the official. Kashin Kakazu was a rascal. Born Kame Kakazu and the third son of farmers, my grandfather managed to skip school because he and his sister had the same name. School officials thus believed that there was only one Kame Kakazu and never questioned the whereabouts of the boy child. "I hated school," recalled my grandfather, "and played all day." When he left Okinawa for Hawaii, he assumed the name of his elder brother, Kamesuke, to gain admittance, because he was underage, and boldly informed the immigration officials that his sister, Kame, who was sixteen years old at the time, was his wife because laborers with wives were preferred over single men. Upon arrival in Honolulu, my grandfather and his sister were recruited to work at Ewa Plantation on the island of Oahu. Three years later he arranged his sister's marriage, but she died of a fever shortly thereafter.

My grandfather's ploy was a variation of a wider practice called *kari fufu*, or "temporary spouse." Women and men agreed to become temporary spouses to gain entry into Hawaii, and after having been admitted, they applied for a divorce and later married someone else. Takayo Iwamoto went to Hawaii when she was sixteen years old as the *kari fufu* of a family friend. She later married Nobuichi Ishimoto. An *issei* woman whispered to researcher Barbara F. Kawakami, "You ask me if I came as a picture bride. Not really. I came to Hawaii as a kari fufu. So, actually, this is my second marriage. But I hardly knew the man I came to Hawaii with. I do not even remember his name. We parted as soon as we got here."[21]

Whatever the means, my grandfather managed to claim his bride, and the two rode by taxi from Honolulu to the outskirts of the town and beyond, far beyond, into the countryside. My grandmother's spirits dropped as the taxi pulled up to an irrigation camp on the Waipahu Plantation. The forlorn row of shacks, she remembered, was surrounded by seemingly endless fields of cane that shielded from view the outside world. She had no friends and shared the one-room, wooden structure with a man she hardly knew. Many nights, my grandmother said, she spent crying quietly to herself as she listened to the heavy breathing of her stranger-husband. She could not gain solace by writing to her parents, she explained, because if she told them of her extreme loneliness, they would be worried, and she could not bring them needless sorrow. So she cried alone, in the dark.

I wonder if my grandmother ventured far outside the camp that confined her to seek the high ground where she could rise above the fields of cane and see the horizon beyond? She must have quickly exhausted the possibilities of the camp, its communal toilets and bath, its outdoor kitchens, and its six families and several bachelors. She must have followed the stream that flowed from the mountains, discovered the guavas and mangoes that grew along its bank, and smiled at the sight of the bright red lehua flower that bloomed only in the higher elevations where cooler winds blew. She might have even ascended Koolau's slopes, so high, so far away from

21. Ibid., pp. 12–13.

her isolation that, breathless, she might have gained a glimpse of the blue, shimmering Pacific Ocean that stretched into the distance, lapping on friendlier shores.

But plantation labor did not allow for dreams or dreamers, and heterosexual relations resulted in pregnancies and babies as surely as the shrill whistle blew every morning, save Sunday, to call the workers out to the fields. My grandmother did not have time to ponder her destiny. Her life of labor was interrupted only for the bearing and births of eleven children, six girls and five boys, which became almost a biennial ritual. She originally wanted four or five children, my grandmother said, but more hands were useful for farming and brought in added income for the household. Still, she worried about the children's education, and because the family was so poor, her daughters, particularly the older ones, had to stop their schooling to care for the younger ones and find salaried jobs. My grandmother, like so many other picture brides, worked in the field and in the home, bearing the burden of self, family, and community. They were not merely bold; they were strong.

"There were mostly picture brides on the ship—young girls, couples, men who came to Japan to find brides," remembered Ai Miyasaki. "Filipinos were on board also. The picture brides were full of ambition, expectation, and dreams. None knew what their husbands were like except by the photos. I wondered how many would be saddened and disillusioned. There were many. The grooms were not what the women thought they were. The men would say that they had businesses and send pictures which were taken when they were younger and deceived the brides. In reality, the men carried blanket rolls on their backs and were farm laborers. The men lied about their age and wrote they were fifteen years younger than they actually were."[22]

The migrants encountered other kinds of lies. Both in Japan and in America, they met unscrupulous guides, translators, hotel owners, immigration officials, and sailors, who preyed upon their naivete and vulnerability. "When I landed in Victoria, Canada, in 1903," said Ichijiro Tanaka, "a Japanese came up to me. 'Since you cannot speak English, you cannot enter. I'll arrange for you to enter temporarily.' So saying, he put me in a Japanese inn in the city. The people at the inn were very kind, yet I felt completely helpless. A couple of days later the same man came back again and said, 'Since I have taken care of things for you at the Immigration Office,

22. Sarasohn, *Issei*, pp. 55–56.

you now can enter the country.' I gave my $10 to him. The man looked like he wanted more, but at the time it was all I had. It was not only I who was cheated like this, but quite a number of others also."[23]

According to Ray Muramoto of Seattle, husbands whose picture brides were detained by immigration officials were the most susceptible to paying bribes, because they had already paid substantial amounts to secure their brides and bring them over, and because they faced additional passage costs if the women were returned to Japan. "Therefore the grooms made every effort to get their brides out of the detention houses, even using bribery," charged Muramoto. "As far as I know, the highest price I heard of was $100 for one bride. Instead of giving the money directly to the Immigration Office, the groom passed it through the innkeepers."[24]

Japanese racism spawned yet another kind of lie. Baishiro Tamashiro remembered talking to several Japanese women in about 1905 who believed that Okinawans had tails. The Ryuku Islands were an independent kingdom until 1609, when they were conquered by the Tokugawa shogunate. Japanese commonly held that Okinawans were hairier, darker skinned, and inferior to them. "They looked down on Okinawans," he said, "therefore we had much hostility. . . . They would say Okinawans are just nothing." In 1906, while waiting in Yokohama to board the ship that would take him to Hawaii, Tamashiro and his fellow Okinawans were fed the rice from the previous night's meal mixed with the fresh rice that was left over after the Japanese had eaten. "It was sour and we could not eat it," he recalled. Tamashiro protested against this discriminatory practice at the inn, and he ultimately won his case.[25]

In America, racism and sexism sometimes greeted the migrants. Fuyo Nishiyori remembered her reception by a health inspector in 1905. She and her traveling companions, three young women, all graduates of Aoyama Gakuin University, were treated by the official as if they were prostitutes or diseased women. "The inspector said, 'Smell bad! Don't come too close!'" recalled Nishiyori. "I was upset at being treated like a dirty pig. There, while we held in front of us a slate bearing our names, a photo was taken. Then the inspector felt our joints at both elbows, around the neck, and on both sides of the groin. Of course it was done while we were fully dressed, but I felt insulted and became furious. This examination was for syphilis only. . . ."[26]

23. Ito, *Issei*, p. 48.
24. Ibid., p. 50.
25. Ethnic Studies Oral History Project, *Uchinanchu: A History of Okinawans in Hawaii* (Honolulu: Ethnic Studies Program, University of Hawaii, 1981), pp. 358, 359.
26. Ito, *Issei*, p. 16.

"My first impression of San Francisco was bad," said Nisuke Mitsumori. "It was March or April of 1905 when I landed in San Francisco. A man from a Japanese inn was at the port to meet me with a one-horse carriage. There was a gang of scoundrels who came to treat the immigrants roughly as soon as they heard that some Japanese had docked." The group of about fifteen to twenty youth gathered around the migrants, shouting abuses at them. "As we went along," explained Mitsumori, "we were bombarded with abuses such as 'Japs,' 'lewd,' et cetera. They even picked horse dung off the street and threw it at us. I was baptized with horse dung. This was my very first impression of America."[27]

Although their departures almost always resulted in separations, the migrants made new friends and conjured up fictive kin—"like brothers and sisters"—having shared a common ordeal and close quarters—"we were third-class passengers"—and their arrival in Hawaii and on the U.S. mainland frequently reunited friends and family members. "I came to San Francisco on September 21, 1912, because my father asked me to come join him in the United States," explained Masuo Akizuki. "When I left Japan, my mother told me to help my father, and I promised her that he would come home within five years." Although Akizuki's father returned to Japan within five years, the younger Akizuki remained in the United States, his promise to his mother kept.[28]

For many Japanese migrants, Hawaii was the first landfall and the place of decision to remain in the islands, return to Japan, or sail eastward to the mainland. My paternal grandfather, Sanguemon Okihiro, left Hiroshima for Hawaii in 1906 to work on a sugar plantation. His picture bride, Taka Nogami, joined him around 1915 and gave birth to my father, Tetsuo, the following year. Taka, with her infant son, returned to Japan in 1917 to care for her mother, who had fallen ill, and later rejoined her husband in Hawaii, where she gave birth to two more sons, Shogo and Takeo. When his elder brother died in a coal-mining accident on the U.S. mainland, Sanguemon moved his family back to Hiroshima to care for his father, Yosaku, on the family farm. Hawaii, for my paternal grandparents, was simply a place of migratory labor. But for my maternal grandparents, the islands were both a place of migratory labor and a place called home. In the words of an Okinawan song, they grew deep roots and green leaves.

27. Sarasohn, *Issei*, p. 59.
28. Steven Misawa, ed., *Beginnings: Japanese Americans in San Jose* (San Jose: Japanese American Community Senior Service, 1981), p. 12.

MY MOTHER DEAR

(A Dialogue)

Let me take my leave, my mother.
Earn money and come home, my child,
As I stay home and pray to the gods.
To this Hawaii from the far away Okinawa
We have come all the way for the sake of money.
Thinking it'd only be a few years we came,
But we have now grown our roots deep and with green leaves.[29]

Japanese laborers sang a kind of blues called *hole hole bushi*. The term derived from the Hawaiian word for stripping leaves off the cane stalk, *hole hole*, combined with the Japanese word for "tune," *bushi*. The tunes were usually Japanese folksongs, and the words were the spontaneous feelings and expressions of workers engaged in plantation labor. Misa Toma called her songs *setsunabushi*, or "songs of pain":

Starting out so early
Lunches on our shoulders
Off to our holehole work
Never seems to be enough.[30]

"I went to Hawi Plantation in Kohala on the Big Island where my younger brother was," remembered Tokushin Nakamoto. "There were many plantations in Kohala, but Hawi was famous for hard work so the pay was a dollar more than other plantations. We were paid $19 a month for 26 days' work. . . . We worked in the sugarcane fields and after the day's work, we slept together in a barrack-like building for single men. There were two or three people living in each room." A woman charged the men for cooking for them, washing their laundry, and mending their clothes. "Many older people went back to Japan because the work was too hard for them," said Nakamoto. "Hawi . . . we had to work very hard."[31]

Baishiro Tamashiro recalled how his hands developed blisters wielding the cane knife at Lihue Plantation on Kauai. "It sure was hard work," he noted. "We had no time to rest. We worked like machines. For 200 of us workers, there were seven

29. Ethnic Studies, *Uchinanchu*, p. xi.
30. From Franklin S. Odo's manuscript collection of unpublished *hole hole bushi*.
31. Ethnic Studies, *Uchinanchu*, pp. 392–93.

or eight *lunas* and above them was a field boss on a horse. We were watched constantly."[32] Tsuru Yamauchi shared Tamashiro's view of the White overseers. "If we thought the *lunas* were coming," she said, "we were afraid. . . . The *lunas* might or might not come once in a day, but we were always scared that they'd come. We couldn't understand their speech, and so we couldn't answer at all. Both men and women worked very hard, because we were scared."[33] A *hole hole bushi* lamented the shattered dream that was Hawaii.

> Wonderful Hawaii, or so I heard.
> One look and it seems like Hell.
> The manager's the Devil and
> His lunas are demons.[34]

But Tokushin Nakamoto held a different opinion of the overseers. "There were some strict supervisors," he conceded but added, "actually, they were not really that bad. They just scolded those who did not work hard, and watched us so we were not lazy. They were very good at their job; they were just strict." The *lunas*, he explained, followed only those who were "lazy or could not work fast," but they did not closely watch those who worked diligently.[35] Of course, the overseers, like the workers, were individuals with personalities and wills, and the discipline they exerted varied from plantation to plantation. Still, as a boy living on Aiea Plantation, I remember the fear the *lunas* inspired in me, perhaps transmitted by my grandparents and parents, or by my experiences in the cane fields, where we hid whenever we saw the dust rise from the dirt road in the wake of the *luna*'s truck. The overseers were policemen, who watched and meted out instant punishment, sometimes with their leather whips.

Because *lunas* were the most immediate and visible personification of oppression on the plantation, they were the frequent targets of abused workers. In November 1892, at Ewa Plantation, more than 200 laborers marched to Honolulu to demand the firing of an overseer who had helped a fellow *luna* ward off an attack by workers; in June 1893, at Kukuihaele, Hawaii, the entire workforce of 250 struck and walked to Honokaa to attend the trial of an overseer who had shot and wounded a Japa-

32. Ibid., p. 360.
33. Ibid., p. 488.
34. Odo and Urata, "Hole Hole Bushi," p. 72.
35. Ethnic Studies, *Uchinanchu*, p. 393.

nese; in January 1894, at Koloa, Kauai, 150 chased a *luna* who had beaten a laborer; in November 1894 and again in January 1895, at Kahuku, Oahu, over 100 workers struck and marched to Honolulu to protest *luna* cruelty and mistreatment; and in November 1897, at Ewa, Oahu, 81 struck over an overseer who had broken a worker's arm. In 1904 on Waipahu Plantation, more than 1,000 laborers struck over the lottery operation run by head *luna* Patterson and his overseers wherein workers were forced to buy tickets, and a few months later, they struck again, demanding the removal of a Japanese overseer, Suyehiro.[36]

Tokusuke Oshiro recalled some of the tactics he and his fellow workers employed to get back at perceived oppression. While supposedly working in the cane fields, they played a game of sickle throwing, gambled, and carried the "corpse" of someone who played dead. "We felt strongly against the plantation and wanted to make trouble for them," he said. "There were weeds . . . which we were supposed to dig, but instead of doing that, we cut the tops off and covered them with soil."[37] Workers also broke tools, pretended to be sick, were slack at their work, and started fires that destroyed the young cane. Although those behaviors might be seen as self-centered and antisocial, they were calculated to even the exploitation balance sheet by damaging the property of the planters and by reducing worker productivity. Laborers also engaged in collective work action, in strikes, that resulted in millions of dollars in losses and virtually shut down sugar production on the island of Oahu in 1909 and 1920.

While workers as a class contested the power of the planters and their allies, women struggled to remove the patriarchal fetters that tied them to men and the household. "Early in the morning, I wouldn't go by myself when I went over to the kitchen, which was separate from the house," explained Tsuru Yamauchi. "At first even to start the fire I brought my husband along. That was because it was uncivilized in those days, you know. Since there were so few women, there were many men who might harass us. The hardest thing to get used to was the bachelors saying this and that. I hated it, no matter what, really, I didn't get used to people."[38] Yamauchi's fears arose from the social reality in which women were the property of men. Choki Oshiro told about a woman who was kidnapped from a plantation camp by a "tough

36. Okihiro, *Cane Fires*, pp. 42–44.
37. Ethnic Studies, *Uchinanchu*, p. 386.
38. Ibid., p. 489.

and violent" man and taken to a hotel room in Honolulu. "She was locked in there," he said. "So we told him we wouldn't have a grudge or any hard feeling against him if he apologized and willingly agreed to send her back to her husband. He agreed and we took her back with us."[39]

Perhaps because of the abuse they suffered at the hands of men, some women might have developed a callous attitude toward them. Ko Shigeta recalled living in the workers' barracks on Aiea Plantation. "Fifty of us, both bachelors and married couples," he observed, "lived together in a humble shed—a long ten-foot wide hallway made of wattle and lined along the sides with a slightly raised floor covered with a grass rug, and two *tatami* mats to be shared among us. We also shared the same bathing facilities; while I was washing myself the wives of the others stepped over me matter-of-factly, as if I were a dog or cat in their path." He concluded with the richly evocative: "I remember the cold drops from the ends of their hair falling on my back."[40]

Although work outside the home afforded women greater freedoms through their wider social interactions and their earned incomes, it subjected them to additional burdens because their husbands rarely shared the responsibilities for domestic labor. Tsuru Yamauchi remembered how she watered the cane before sunrise, while it was still dark, and later joined her husband at weeding. "Everyone worked in rows when we hoed in the fields," she said. "Where husband and wife were allowed to work together, I worked with him. That's where married couples worked, and each couple moved from one place to another." After ten hours of field work, Yamauchi prepared dinner for the family, washed the dishes, and put the children to bed. "At night after having the children go to bed, and having taken my bath close to bedtime, I did the children's ironing, trying not to make much noise. They could hear everything, you know; the walls were so close to each other. It was 10 o'clock when I went to bed."[41]

Taga Toki described her mornings, making lunches for the twenty bachelors who worked with her husband. "I got up at 3:00 A.M. . . . My second baby often woke up and cried, so I strapped him to my back to do the cooking. The rice was cooked in a large Chinese pot with a heavy lid, on an open fire outdoors. . . . Every morning, I lined up the double-decker bento cans—twenty of them—and filled them with rice, a piece of fish, and pickles."[42] A *hole hole bushi* captured a hassled mother's day:

39. Ibid., p. 415.
40. Ito, *Issei*, p. 21.
41. Ethnic Studies, *Uchinanchu*, pp. 493–95.
42. Kawakami, *Japanese Immigrant Clothing*, p. 129.

It's starting to pour
There goes my laundry
My baby is crying
And the rice just burned.[43]

Even as women's labor both within and without the household enabled the economic viability of the *issei* family, women's nurturing promoted the emotional well-being of *issei* men. Alone in a sea of cane, Choki Oshiro waited for the water from the reservoir above to course its way through the irrigation ditches to where he stood below. "I heard a sound like human footsteps walking through the cane field," he recalled. "I looked up wondering who it could be. To my surprise it was my grandmother in her everyday clothes. I called 'Grandma!' then she disappeared. Three months after this incident, I received a letter informing me of her death. She must have been worried and wanted to see for herself how I was doing in Hawaii. She came to see me that night in the cane field and probably was relieved because I was well and doing fine. I cried, thinking of her deep and beautiful love. Whenever I remembered this, I cried in gratitude."[44]

Living in Hawaii, one was always confronted with the sea. The volcanic rocks and sandy beaches that ring the island both defined the limits of livelihood and possibilities and provided a vantage point from which to survey the seemingly endless sea. The view from the shore was colored by mainland labor recruiters, who sought to entice plantation workers with promises of higher wages and better opportunities on the West Coast. "The laborers will be subjected to no delay upon arriving in San Francisco, but can get work immediately," a 1905 advertisement pledged. "Employment offered in picking strawberries and tomatoes, planting beets, mining, and domestic service. Now is the time to go! Wages $1.50 a day." When plantation salaries stood at about $16 a month, the prospect of doubling one's income at labor that appeared less onerous than cane cultivation apparently stimulated a considerable exodus of Japanese workers from the islands.[45]

Typical of many Japanese migrants during the early twentieth century along the West Coast, Sadame Inouye's work pattern was cut from the older cloth worn by Chinese laborers in the fields and orchards, forests and waters, mines and rail-

43. Odo, unpublished *hole hole bushi*.
44. Ethnic Studies, *Uchinanchu*, p. 409.
45. Okihiro, *Cane Fires*, pp. 36–37.

115

roads of the American West. Inouye stayed in Hawaii for two days, got his passport stamped there, and landed in San Francisco. Staying only the night, he boarded a boat for a Japanese work camp on an island near Stockton on the Sacramento River. "First we worked in the onion fields for a month or so," recalled Inouye. "Then we went to a neighboring island to dig potatoes. It was about August when we finished the job and came up to Sacramento to work until the middle of September, when we went to pick grapes." During winter, there was little work, and Inouye had to wait until spring to go to San Leandro, where he picked green peas and planted tomatoes. In June and July, he and several others chopped down trees and cleared the field of stumps for fifty cents per tree. "When I worked here and there," he noted, "I carried my own blanket roll with me and slept where I could. Sometimes I stayed in boarding houses." In the fall, Inouye headed south to Naples near Santa Barbara, where he briefly worked in a railroad section gang until he ran away to Santa Ana to cut celery. After celery season, he picked strawberries in Gardena and eventually worked for a Japanese farmer in Venice for about six months.[46]

Unlike plantation work in Hawaii, migratory labor on the mainland involved frequent movement, following the seasonal offering of work. In agriculture, the pattern was commonly dictated by the times when crops were ready for harvest. Accordingly, Japanese farm laborers picked strawberries at the northern end of California's Santa Clara Valley from April to June, moved to the middle and southern end of the valley to pick apricots and prunes in July and August, traveled south to Fresno to pick grapes in the late summer, and returned to northern California to winter in towns like San Jose, Stockton, and Sacramento.[47]

"Back in those days, the situation was especially terrible for the Japanese, whether here in the United States or over there in Japan," observed Juhei Kono. "The houses where they lived were just like chicken coops, narrow and small, and looked like remodeled stables. It was true in California too. I often used to visit Brawley in the Imperial Valley of California. Japanese people in that area lived just like that. Once their land lease expired, they had a horse pull their house and move it on to another field to work."[48] A newspaper reporter filed this report after visiting a Japanese labor camp near Fresno. "The camps are worse than dog and pig pens," he wrote. "They are totally unfit for human beings to sleep in. . . . No one, not even dirt-poor peas-

46. Sarasohn, *Issei*, pp. 76–78.
47. Timothy J. Lukes and Gary Y. Okihiro, *Japanese Legacy: Farming and Community Life in California's Santa Clara Valley* (Cupertino: California History Center, 1985), pp. 21–26.
48. Sarasohn, *Issei*, p. 75.

ants, wants to live in such unpleasant and filthy surroundings. These camps are the reason why so many robust workers become ill and die."[49]

Kane Kozono left Japan to join her husband in California and accompanied him in his search for employment. They first lived in Alameda, where he worked as a gardener and she worked as a domestic servant of a White family. "I was getting used to life in this country by then and doing fine in Alameda," she said. "I was paid five dollars a week for the housework I was doing there. . . . I was settling into the life there fairly well, but we moved to Sacramento, where some of my husband's relatives were working on a farm. My husband started growing onions, and together with a friend of ours, I worked there digging onions, putting them in a sack, and so forth. I was young then and could do the hard work." But Kozono also cooked for the field hands and bore and reared her children. "After I had babies, raising children was another big job. Whenever I went to work, I took them with me to the ranch, and I would leave them sleeping under a tree. . . . And when the day's work was over, I would carry one of them on my back to our home. Men had to work only while they were out in the field," pointed out Kozono, "whereas I had to do all those things besides my share of work in the field. I did their laundry after work too. It was a really grueling, hard time for me."[50]

Gin Okazaki remembered listening to her future husband in Japan tell "dream-like stories about America." On board the ship, as a nineteen-year-old bride, Okazaki's mind was "more flaming with expectations of a new world than with anticipation of seeing my newly-married husband again," she confessed. But she was shocked by the reality of farming life in Washington. Okazaki fetched water from a well, and they had no bath. "We heated the water and bathed in a tub," she recalled. "There was no electricity; we used lamps. Even backward Japan was not so bad as this. It was really living in some God-forsaken place. But my husband and I toiled on, sweating all over." Okazaki and her husband delivered their children, four girls and four boys. "At the time we knew about family planning," she said. "But since we had been taught that women naturally should give birth to many babies, we didn't think of using artificial birth control." Although they toiled together in the fields, Okazaki worked alone within the household. "My husband was a Meiji man; he didn't even glance at the house work or child care," she explained. "No matter how busy I was,

49. Ichioka, *Issei*, p. 83.
50. Sarasohn, *Issei*, pp. 83–84.

he would never change a diaper. It may sound strange, but Issei women on the immigrant frontier devoted themselves to their husbands. At mealtime, if the food was scarce, the husband ate plenty first, and we were satisfied with the left-overs."[51]

Kimiko Ono described a typical workday on her tomato farm. Before sunrise, Ono and her husband awakened and picked the day's tomato harvest until about 6:30 A.M., when she prepared breakfast and woke up the children and they all sat down at the breakfast table as a family. Her husband then took the tomatoes to market, while Ono, taking her three children with her to the greenhouse, watered and tended the tomato plants. "Even when the children were tired of playing and fussed, I couldn't quit and go to them," she recalled sadly. "Meanwhile the crying voices would stop, and many times I found my youngsters sleeping on the ground. Telling myself, 'Poor little things! When you grow up I will let you do whatever you want to do . . . only please forgive your mama now. . . .' I worked continually." Her husband returned about 7 P.M., and she made dinner and put the children to bed. She sorted tomatoes and packed them in boxes until about midnight if she had finished early. Ono was also a poet. She wrote

> Both my hands grimy,
> Unable to wipe away
> The sweat from my brow,
> Using one arm as towel—
> That was I . . . working . . . working.[52]

Japanese migrant workers sojourned as far north as Alaska, where they performed seasonal work in the salmon and whale canneries and prospected for gold. The "Alaska boys," as they were called, left Seattle for the salmon season, which extended from April to August. Kibun Miyazaki was one of those Alaska boys, who had wandered from job to job up and down the West Coast, "from Seattle to Wapato, Brahma, Rose Inlet in Alaska, Everett, to the north of Bellingham, Blaine, Yakima, North Yakima, again to Wapato and Seattle, and finally to Los Angeles." Miyazaki graduated only from middle school but was fluent in Japanese, English, and French, and his close friend described him as "a thinker" who was not accepted by

51. Ito, *Issei*, pp. 249-50.
52. Ibid., pp. 279-81.

118

White American society, despite his manifest abilities, and who died young. While in Alaska in 1916, Miyazaki reflected upon his immediate circumstances.

"Rose Inlet is a place where everything is green. . . . It is really a wild and Alaska-like place," he wrote to his friend. "The building of the cannery which buys our labor for one summer stands on a piece of cleared land on the rocky shore which appears as a piece of nature unchanged since times immemorial. The Indian houses there remind me of something to be found at the back end of tenement houses in Japan. And that's all there is to Rose Inlet. In front of our camp the sea-water overflows the deep sound, and around the sound huge rocks expose their rough surfaces here and there, and high mountains half covered with snow rise steeply, scraping the sky." Set against that timeless grandeur of nature was the mundane, the banal, that scarred the landscape like the cannery that bought his labor for a season. The workers, he told his friend, were like young men everywhere. "They find a focus for their interest in the commonplace life—women, alcohol and dirty stories. They laugh slyly over such things, and it seems utterly absurd to me." But even daily existence can induce visions that transcend time and place. Although the food was "quite satisfactory," he wrote, "the real feast in the camp is the bath we make every day. I can look out at the ocean while I take a bath. I cannot see the gulls flying without recalling from old memories the hot springs spa in my home town."[53]

Cold. The waters of the deep, surging sound and the winds that whipped around the majestic, snow-capped mountains must have been icy cold. Cold. The words and deeds of the "traveling birds," the men who lived shiftless lives, must have struck Miyazaki as being cold, keenly cold, and devoid of reason and humanity. Cold. The cannery and Indian dwellings, the long hours of labor from 6 A.M. to 6 P.M., and the mind-numbing work of making 50,000 cases of cans and cutting through salmon "piled high like a mountain" must have seemed cold, bitterly cold to the young intellectual. That sense of futility and transience was expressed in his poem:

> Gulls . . . and again the tears.
> July rain falling on the sound,
> Summer deepening,

53. Ibid., pp. 365–66.

> And now that fishing village
> Where we too spend a season.

But there was also warmth, emanating from the commonplace, the utter absurdity, the "facts of life in camp." Gulls took wing and soared above the wild, Alaskan place; like memories that had no boundaries they ascended, and Miyazaki, in the warm bath, looked out westward across the sea, sparkling in the late-summer sun, to the hot springs spa in his hometown. Miyazaki offered the following counterpoint to summer's end.

> These mountains are cast
> In silent melancholy.
> Nor will I lament
> In view of their stature,
> Faced with their tranquility.[54]

Amid the cold, there was warmth.

54. Ibid., pp. 366–67.

As the sun rose above the Inyo and White Mountains to the east, and ascended the sky, casting shadows and dispelling some of the morning mist, I continued my search through the remains of Manzanar. Hearing voices amid the silence, I agreed with a former resident of this camp, Jeanne Wakatsuki Houston, who would later reflect upon her return to Manzanar: "It was so characteristically Japanese, the way lives were made more tolerable by gathering loose desert stones and forming with them something enduringly human," she wrote of her fellow internees and their labor of love in arranging stones and dry, desert wood to form gardens near the doors of their barracks. "Each stone," she noted, "was a mouth, speaking for a family, for some man who had beautified his doorstep."[1]

We had spread out to explore the ruins, when my wife, Libby, called out to me: "Come over here. See what I've found." There in front of her, arching upward, was a gnarled tree trunk, bearing the bends and scars of years of desert wind, cold and heat, years of human neglect. The trunk bore branches that reached outward, ever outward, and on their tips, fluttering in the breeze, were exquisite, fragile cherry blossoms. I shall never forget that sight. Someone must have planted this tree, I knew. Someone must have had faith in the future, I thought. Someone must have believed in her or his humanity, I felt. Spring had come to Manzanar.

James Shinkai, a *nisei* journalist, wrote about time's passage at Manzanar in an untitled poem.

1. Out of the desert's bosom, storm swept with wind and dust,
   Out of smiles and curses, of tears and cries forlorn;
   Mixed with broken laughter, forced because they must;
   Toil, sweat and bleeding wounds, red and raw and torn.
   Out on the desert's bosom—a new town is born.

2. Dust clouds, like brown smoke, rose and swirl and blow
   From hidden lairs in icy crags, towering high,
   Like hungry pack of wolves, the gale sweeps low,
   Fangs sharp and bared, shrieking to the sky;
   The guardian peaks emerge, serene and high.

1. Jeanne Wakatsuki Houston and James D. Houston, *Farewell to Manzanar* (Boston: Houghton Mifflin, 1973), p. 137.

3. Summer, with long, parched nights and days;
   And heaven's bowl a shimmering blue of heat;
   The thirsty hills are choked. The sun's hot blaze
   Before encroaching autumn, once more retreats.
   King Winter reigns upon his icy seat.

4. A year is gone. A quickening in the air;
   The desert stirs beneath the freshening rain.
   The scent of sage, the wild rose perfume rare,
   The tumbling brooks break forth in glad refrain;
   Another Spring—perhaps new hope, new life again.[2]

Japanese farmers along the West Coast held annual picnics, usually in the spring to commemorate the warming breezes and to view the budding fruit trees. Families living in adjacent farm clusters enjoyed the day together, commonly taking their lunch baskets and blankets to spread under the orchard trees to enjoy the fragrance and beauty of the blossoms: apricots and apples, plums and cherries. Others chose open fields, where they could run races, strain at tug-of-war ropes, and hold *sumo* wrestling contests. V. Ishikawa remembered the occasion: "We always went to the foothills for the picnics," she said. "We went to the same ranch, it belonged to a farmer, one Japanese family used to live and work on his place. . . . everybody had their own lunches, you know *bento*. . . . The games . . . we always just ran. . . . The parents all ran too, the old ladies did spoon races where they run and carry something in a spoon and try not to drop it. The prizes were very menial, pencils, tablets . . . and we were glad to get the pencils, we didn't get much in those days, it was really something."[3]

The annual spring picnic was a time for people, members of a community, to shake off the quiescence of winter, put on their finery as if to complement the exuberance of spring, and renew friendships and enmities. People sat in groups, exchanged stories and argued, ate and drank, laughed and cried. G. Fujita remembered: "We'd go all the way over near Shaver Lake. The family would take the old model T and oh, we had a big time. All day Sunday. We wanted to get away from all the people because the first generation wanted to get drunk. . . . That was the

2. Sue Kunitomi Embrey, *The Lost Years, 1942–1946* (Los Angeles: Moonlight Publications, 1972), p. 44.

3. David Mas Masumoto, *Country Voices: The Oral History of a Japanese American Family Farm Community* (Del Rey, Calif.: Inaka Countryside Publications, 1987), pp. 100–101.

sole reason they went way up there where there was nobody, that was the main reason. The men sang and clapped . . . just the men, they were rowdy ones. The women watched and took care of the kids."[4]

Customarily, a formal photograph was taken of the picnic revelers. A typical picture from the 1920s and 1930s would show virtually all the women and girls wearing white spring dresses, long-sleeved and descending nearly to their ankles, with hats to ward off the sun, and nearly all the men and boys dressed in white shirts, some with collars unbuttoned, others with ties, and long trousers, topped with hats for men and caps for boys. Unforgettable are the faces in the photographs—the faces of women, men, and children. Children, the very notion of them seemed unthinkable a few decades earlier, when procreation was effectively precluded by practice and law. Japanese patriarchy discouraged women's migration and encouraged their prostitution, American antimiscegenation laws prevented interracial unions, and, in 1921, the United States urged and Japan agreed to stop issuing passports to picture brides.

But positioned prominently in the pictures were the children, the second generation, who were by birth U.S. citizens, and as citizens could not be as easily denied the privileges of life, liberty, and property as their first-generation parents. American law rendered the *issei* (and Asians generally) "aliens ineligible for citizenship," based on the 1790 Naturalization Act, which limited those who could become U.S. citizens—or the "worthy part of mankind" in the words of the act—to free White persons and Africans in 1870. Cast as perpetual foreigners, the first generation could not participate in electoral politics and, throughout much of the West, were denied ownership of real property. Aliens ineligible for citizenship, California's 1913 Alien Land Law stated, were forbidden to own land, and its 1920 version prohibited them from leasing land. But the second generation could not be so easily dismissed, and their birth and legal status, accordingly, were instrumental in the renewal of Japanese America.

The process of transformation from Japanese to Japanese American was ongoing, persistent, and multifaceted. It was not simply linear or teleological; it did not move toward a single object or goal. Instead, becoming Japanese American was a matter neither of resisting nor of accepting all change, of remaining "pure" Japanese or old country or of becoming 100 percent American or new country, reduced

4. Ibid., pp. 99-100.

to traditional or modern, the first generation or second generation. Becoming Japanese American was directed simultaneously by external forces that said who you were and who you were not, and by internal forces that resisted and accepted those intrusions while conjuring up alternatives that were self-propelled. Becoming Japanese Ameican was not dramatic, discontinuous, or sudden; it was not subtle, natural, or given. Rather the process was struggled over in the everyday, ordinary lives of the people who made Japanese America.

"Married in 1913, I landed in Tacoma following my husband who had gone to the States just one step ahead of me," said Sakiko Suyama. "First of all we bought outfits of Western clothes at Hara's. When I landed I was in a kimono with a maroon-colored pleated over-skirt, my hair arranged in a bun." Suyama recalled squeezing into a corset for the first time. "The corset was so tight that women couldn't bend over. I had to ask my husband to tie my shoe strings!" She described herself dressed in Western clothes. "I, in a big hat and high laced shoes, wearing a high-necked blouse and trailing skirt belted and buckled at the waist—and of course for the first time in my life a brassier and a bustle (hip-pad). The trouble was the underwear! Japanese women were only accustomed to use petticoats. Wearing Western panties for the first time, I frequently forgot to pull them down when I went to the toilet so I often got them wet."[5]

Yoshito Fujii described the picture brides who arrived in Seattle. "Many stayed in my brother's Fujii Hotel," she remembered. "A lot of young men came up from Sacramento to meet their brides. I couldn't tell who were farmers and who weren't, for all were dressed dandily. They even wore white gloves. . . . The brides came here in their kimono. As soon as they got here, they were taken to the Abe Dress Shop, which was close to our hotel, to buy Western-style dresses. You can walk on the street in kimono without feeling embarrassed these days," Fujii explained. "At that time, it was too embarrassing to do so. The Japanese ladies looked different and beautiful in Western-style dresses. Some put their shoes on backwards and couldn't move well, for it was their first time to wear such clothing."[6]

Western dress was supposed to give cover to both the gendered and the racialized body, thereby rendering the Japanese invisible, indistinguishable from the rest of America. But sometimes the *issei* appropriated Western dress in ways that achieved

5. Ito, *Issei*, p. 249.
6. Sarasohn, *Issei*, p. 107.

just the opposite effect. Riyo Orite told the story of Japanese women who had returned to Japan from the United States and had given their Western clothing to
women who were leaving for America. Some of those garments included lace underwear that the women found to be so beautiful that they wore them outside their
dresses, thinking that they would display them prominently. "We found out after
we got to the hotel," she sighed. "The hotel owner's wife was surprised and laughed
at those ladies when we got there. She was amazed, 'How daring you are to have
traveled in such a fashion!'"[7]

In another twist, Japanese women in Hawaii took the *momohiki* (breeches or
pantaloons) worn over the kimono in Japan while doing farm work and wore it
under their full skirts, adapted from Hawaiian, Portuguese, and Spanish women,
to cover their bodies from the waist down while working in the sugar fields. Both
Japanese men and women modified their Japanese clothing for work in Hawaii's
plantations. But women were more selective than men in their borrowing of clothing design and materials, and strove to wear clothing that was practical but that also
typified their ethnicity and distinguished them from other ethnic groups, according
to dressmaker and scholar Barbara F. Kawakami.[8] Even work clothing, thus, became
an expression of ethnic identity.

Japanese women wore a sash around their waists to hold their jackets, probably
copied from the Chinese, and skirts in place. The sash was usually made of black
cotton cloth and was about eighteen inches wide and two-and-a-half yards long. Its
counterpart in Japanese culture was the *obi*, worn with the kimono, and a symbol of
womanhood. An *issei* woman explained the use and meaning of the sash in Hawaii:
"The long black sash was used mainly for the purpose of holding the jacket and skirt
firmly in place," she began. "We were so used to wearing an obi back in the village
that the wide sash tightly wound around our waist gave us a feeling of assurance and
comfort. . . . It also brought us closer to the village we left behind."[9]

In Seattle, there were several dressmaking schools begun by *issei* women. Isami
Sunohara opened her school in 1919 and attracted students from the city and surrounding communities. "In the early period students were only Issei women, some
of whom brought their children with them, and they all studied hard so that they
could learn to sew Western clothes for their families as well as for a side job," Suno-

7. Ibid., p. 55.
8. Kawakami,
*Japanese Immigrant
Clothing*, pp. 87, 101.
9. Ibid., p. 99.

hara explained. Others were so poor that they managed in part by wearing hand-me-downs. "During that time we could buy three cotton dresses for one dollar," remembered Kimiko Ono. "I only spent one dollar a year for a dress, and sometimes I thankfully received used clothes from my friends." Meanwhile tucked away in their trunks, like precious cultural artifacts, were their kimonos. The poet Shoko observed:

> Lovely kimono,
> I've never worn you, and yet
> Still air you every summer.[10]

Hanayo Inouye recalled how in Japan her mother made kimonos for her. "She made me beautiful kimonos when I became of marriageable age, but I never got to put them on, not even once," Inouye said. "She wanted me to wear them when I became a real bride, you see." Her mother told her: " 'When you become a bride, neighbors will look forward to seeing you wear new kimonos every day. This one today, that one the next day. . . . You have to wait until then.' " But Inouye left for America and never wore her mother's handiwork. "You know, in Japan they have airings of kimonos and other clothes every midsummer," explained Inouye. " 'I was airing your kimonos today,' " her mother wrote to her, " 'and my tears stained parts of them. I'm very sorry.' "[11]

Food, like clothing, was carried to America by the *issei*, but it was also adapted to the necessities and tastes of the new land. Haruko Fukuyama recalled cooking for men at a sawmill. "I was hired to cook for thirty-five or forty people. The pay was $1.00 per person per month. The income averaged $35 a month, without a single day off. I also took care of the washing and made another dollar per person per month." Men also cooked for themselves, especially when there were no women around. Inota Tawa worked in a railroad gang headed by Tadashichi Tanaka, who maintained that Japanese should not eat rice like their fellow Chinese railroad workers but should "live like Americans." "Chinese seemed to have the custom of eating warm rice three times a day," noted Tawa; "at lunchtime they all got together and made a fire, cooked rice and ate it. We Japanese were not supposed to eat rice, and so we had many strange menus. Since bread was expensive and we couldn't af-

10. Ito, *Issei*, pp. 276–77, 280, 283.
11. Sarasohn, *Issei*, p. 116.

128

ford the same foods as whites, we ate dumpling soup for breakfast and supper. We chopped up bacon and fried it, then added potatoes and onions with salted water, and cooked the flour dumplings in that. For lunch we had so-called *bottera* which was something like flour-and-water pancakes cooked in a skillet, and for a side dish we ate cooked soy beans and bacon. We made coffee for lunch, too. It was a strange Western menu that we invented!"[12] The concoction provided a metaphor of the immigrant experience for the poet Ryusei.

> Sticky dumpling soup
> And immigrant episodes,
> Mixed into a stew![13]

Tawa's Japanese companions, however, believed that they ate dumpling soup because "there was no rice and no soy sauce" and thus they used what they could afford and get. Yozan wrote:

> None but Japanese
> Could stand on a foundation
> Of mere dumpling soup![14]

Living on a diet of dumpling soup, Kaneo Kawahara contracted night blindness. His work companions had scolded him, " 'Don't be so extravagant,' " they had told him when he asked for more nutritious food. "After a while I finally became night-blind," said Kawahara. "I couldn't see things in the evening, so I quit working earlier than other people. One day I was standing in front of a shack, alone and lonely. I saw a woman approaching along the railroad from a distance. I felt it was strange and gazed at her, and discovered that the woman was my dear old grandma in my hometown. 'Oh, grandma!' Shouting, I ran toward her—but suddenly she disappeared. I was seized with a sharp homesickness, and in the middle of that wasteland I wept out loud."[15]

At a sawmill camp in Washington, Shoichiro Katsuno reported that Whites spent about 75-85 cents daily on food, whereas the 100-150 Japanese workers could afford only less than half that amount. "The food was Japanese—fifth class rice imported from Japan, dried foods, vegetables, dried radish strips and burdock, lotus root, and

12. Ito, *Issei*, pp. 276, 293-94.

13. Ibid., p. 293.

14. Ibid., pp. 295, 296.

15. Ibid., p. 301.

koyadofu (a dish made from bean curd). For breakfast they served rice and *miso* soup with vermicelli in it. Lunch was rice, and fish and vegetables boiled hard with soy sauce. Once a week they cooked such a mixture with meat in it. They served fish about twice a week. On Sundays we had red bean soup with *mochi* (rice cake). . . . It was impossible to have fresh vegetables or fruits." [16]

For about eight dollars per month, plantation workers in Ewa, Oahu, ate at mess halls, where "meals were extremely poor, with thin Miso soup with noodles in addition to rice," according to a history of migrants from Fukushima. "But this noodle soup was the most popular dish of our supper, and everyone tried hard to scoop as much of the noodle at the bottom of the pot as possible, some trying four or five times to scoop it, with those waiting for their turn shouting 'Hurry up! Hurry up!' For lunch we had rice and soybean paste, but once a week we had rice with a slice of salted salmon or a boiled egg. Some suffered malnutrition and lost their eyesight or died." [17]

Without certain crucial ingredients, the migrants had to improvise. Some men made soy sauce from burnt flour, sugar, salt, and water—"a strange mixture indeed"—and others added wild turnips found along the railroad tracks to their otherwise monotonous dumpling soup. Men working in the far reaches of the forests of the Pacific Northwest hunted deer for meat and invented deer meat sukiyaki. "We couldn't eat the meat just as it was because it was so gamey," explained Hideo Miyazaki, "and at the same time we couldn't preserve it very long. So we cut it up and salted it. Then later we took it out and made it into steak or sukiyaki and got the nourishment from it." [18]

Necessity sometimes induced a smooth blend of what the *issei* brought with them and what they found in America. Workers in Hawaii, for example, commonly made spam sushi, consisting of a slice of canned spam bonded to a rice ball with *nori* (dried, pressed seaweed). The spam was inexpensive, it provided needed protein, and its salty flavor added a tasty counterpoint to the bland rice. Spam sushi, shaped by insufficiency and abject poverty, assumed a funky soul-food status in Hawaii and was appropriated by yuppies (and yappies) in the California of the 1990s, among whom sushi was in and sauerkraut out. Japanese migrants made other tasty combinations. *Nisei* Robert Imagire remembered: "When dad was little, grandma would

16. Ibid., p. 402.
17. Yukiko Kimura, *Issei: Japanese Immigrants in Hawaii* (Honolulu: University of Hawaii Press, 1988), p. 34.
18. Ito, *Issei*, pp. 299, 411–12.

put miso in his Campbell's vegetable soup, to make it taste better." And his daughter, Dorothy Imagire, exclaimed: "My New England husband puts maple syrup on his mochi!"[19]

At other times, the coming together of familiar and novel elicited smiles if not puckered palates. Writer and farmer David Mas Masumoto recounted his attempt to merge California macro organic with Japanese in his brown rice sushi, made of whole-grain brown rice flavored with rice vinegar rolled around vegetable strips and wrapped in a sheet of *nori*. The result was jarring to his grandmother, who upon seeing the brown rice asked, "Ah, did someone burn the rice?" She was used to only polished, white rice called "Japanese rice" as opposed to long-grain "Chinese rice." At a community potluck, Masumoto reported of the brown rice sushi he had brought, "people stopped as they picked up a piece with their chopsticks, and held it up in the light seemingly studying the color. . . . Some were surprised and had wondered why it looked different, others commented on its slightly different flavor."[20]

Shelter, like clothing and food, was negotiated, was worked over by the Japanese in America. The physical structures were almost always predetermined, whether they were shacks in Hawaii's plantation camps, barns and boardinghouses along the West Coast, or urban basements and rural farmhouses throughout the American West. "Our camp was five wooden shelters built of rough boards, where more than 100 immigrants were living, washing clothes, or cooking," recalled Kasaku Yonashiro of a sugar plantation on the island of Hawaii. "The cooking place was outside of the shelter, protected from the rain and wind by empty bags for curtains, and inside the bag curtains was an amusing sight with the rows of more than a hundred empty kerosene cans used as cooking stoves."[21]

Besides cookhouses, plantation camps relied upon communal outhouses arranged in rows and community bathhouses. Noriyu Koga recalled that in his camp, the toilet was about 100 feet from the house. "The toilet was far away," he said. "There was a hole in the ground. You couldn't get there in time. If you had a stomach ache, there wasn't enough time. You had to run." The bath, Koga noted, was a Japanese-style *furo*, where the bathers were supposed to scrub themselves to remove the sweat and dirt before entering the bath. "In the old days, the plantation camp had a bath . . . women's side and men's side," he explained. "In the middle, there was a partition.

19. Quotations from *Home Cooking*, a mixed-media print with *nori* and bay leaves, by Dorothy Imagire, 1993.
20. Masumoto, *Country Voices*, pp. 115–21.
21. Kimura, *Issei*, p. 54.

You were in the same water. Eh, you were dirty. If you did work like *hapai ko* [carrying burnt cane], you were really filthy. After work when you go to the bath, there was no more hot water so you had no choice. . . . But a lot of people used that water. Even if you felt the water was dirty, you had no choice. You had to use that bath."[22]

Yasutaro Soga, newspaper editor and community leader, described plantation housing about the turn of the century. "The living area of the laborers . . . was like a hog pen unfit for human housing," he wrote. "Several hundred men and women lived in shacks built of rough boards white-washed with cement. Each shack was overcrowded, without privacy and with no sanitation facilities. The multitiered bunks were used by single men while a small room was used by a married couple, but they were often compelled to share it with single men. While there was a facility for drinking water, there was no sewage system, and the whole camp stank with an unbearable stench. All the plantations had the same conditions."[23]

At about the same time in San Jose, California, Masuo Akizuki observed that "everybody was working in the countryside. The boarding houses in San Jose Japantown found jobs for us. They brought us by horse carriage to the place to work, and we each were given one blanket. Our living conditions were miserable at that time. We slept next to a horse stable on our blankets and some straw."[24] "Twenty to thirty Japanese sleep alongside each other in fieldsheds on the edge of fruit orchards," a 1903 guide reported of the Fresno area. "These sheds are called camps. There are well built camps as well as makeshift ones. Most of the latter have no beds. Men sleep with bedding on straws spread over dirt floors."[25]

Japanese tenant farmers lived under conditions similar to those of migrant workers. A 1911 government report described Japanese farm homes in California's Santa Clara Valley. "The houses are 'boxed up' of rough boards or 'shakes,' unbattened, unplastered, and not ceiled. In the majority of cases one room serves as living room, kitchen, and dining room, but in some cases a shed-like 'lean-to' is provided for cooking and eating. The floors are uncarpeted and the walls unadorned save for picture advertisements." Those conditions, noted the report, fell far below the housing of White tenant farmers.[26]

Shoichi Fukuda described the house he built in California for his family with fifty

22. Dorothy Ochiai Hazama and Jane Okamoto Komeiji, *Okage Sama De: The Japanese in Hawai'i, 1885–1985* (Honolulu: Bess Press, 1986), p. 70.
23. Kimura, *Issei*, p. 96.
24. Misawa, *Beginnings*, p. 12.
25. Ichioka, *Issei*, p. 83.
26. Lukes and Okihiro, *Japanese Legacy*, p. 32.

dollars worth of lumber. "First, we built a twelve- by twenty-foot floor. Second, we had to have walls. If we built columns at four corners, we would not have enough lumber; so we had to build a house which did not have columns. We arranged the two-by-fours to make four walls and pushed the walls against each other. We nailed down the corners to stabilize them. . . . It was enough to withstand the rain so that the three of us—my wife, my child, and myself—could sleep there." But with no ceiling and a roof consisting of a thin board, the house was "very, very hot" in the summer and "very cold" in the winter, and when the wind blew, it "shook violently." "The wall was full of holes through which the mosquitoes could come in," recalled Fukuda. "We had to paste newspapers on these holes not only to keep mosquitoes out but bees too."[27]

In the cities, Japanese student-workers in San Francisco lived in an area of the city where "all the houses were . . . small and dirty," according to writer Bunzo Washizu. "When I arrived in America," he wrote, "we didn't need addresses to visit Japanese homes. As long as we were told of such-and-such intersecting streets, we always found the houses. We had only to look for basements with sooty curtains to find them. There we invariably found Japanese living in cave-like dwellings." Inside, he continued, "the kitchens were filthy and disorderly to the extreme. . . . All cooking was done on one or two-burner oil stoves. We brewed coffee, toasted bread, and grilled smoked salmon on these oil stoves. Thick, black smoke darkened the rooms, and we were oblivious to the odor which assailed our nostrils."[28]

Improved housing and recreational facilities were among the demands made by the plantation workers who struck for higher wages. The 1909 strike led by Soga and others, for example, was stimulated equally by a desire for comparable wages for comparable work and by a determination to settle permanently in Hawaii. Moto-yuki Negoro, a Honolulu attorney who articulated the rationale for the strike, contrasted in the pages of Soga's *Nippu Jiji* the lot of Japanese laborers, who earned $18 a month and were given "pigstylike homes," with that of Portuguese and Puerto Rican workers, who received $22.50 monthly and lived in "family cottages." Referring to Japanese migrants, Negoro maintained: "it is their hope of years and their silent prayer that they recover the lost liberty of choosing and changing their place

27. Sarasohn, *Issei*, pp. 143–44.
28. Lukes and Okihiro, *Japanese Legacy*, p. 23.

of abode and become a full-fledged man and to be in a position to earn a just reward for their labor." The planters smashed the three-month-old strike by arresting its leaders, evicting strikers from their plantation homes, and hiring scabs.[29]

But in the aftermath of the strike, a Bureau of Labor and Statistics report observed that none of the plantations would have suffered had they undertaken "a little more of what is known as welfare work among the employees," such as "to provide their laborers with recreation amusement, as well as to give them more comfortable and attractive quarters." These included garden plots and recreational areas but also new, improved housing. A 1920 industry letter recommended the building of single-family homes, each having at least two bedrooms and the "necessary wash house, bath house, and other sanitary arrangements" and situated on a 5,000-square-foot lot. Ostensibly, the planters spent over $3 million on remodeling and repairing older buildings, constructing new homes, and working to improve the sanitary facilities between 1922 and 1925.[30]

On the mainland, housing improved with the financial ability of the Japanese to rent or purchase homes and with the availability of tracts that were open to them. One family lived in Little Tokyo, Los Angeles, during the 1920s, moved to a nearby beach community, and returned inland to farm on about twenty acres. Because of California's Alien Land Law, the title to the land could not be held by the *issei* parents but was arranged through a White person, thereby adding to the instability of the family's livelihood and home. The family bought three small buildings that had a total of eight rooms, with one building housing the kitchen, the second, the living room, and the third, living quarters for the workers. But these buildings were portable and were moved from farm to farm, as was common among Japanese farmers at the time.[31] Permanent farm structures that included the farmhouse, barns, sheds, greenhouses, loading docks, and workers' quarters were acquired by the relatively few who had the resources and managed to gain title to the land in the names of their children who were American citizens by birth.

An urban, middle-class family encountered other impediments in housing. Both *issei* parents were highly educated; the father had graduated from trade school, and the mother had graduated from a college in Japan. The man worked for a White firm in Los Angeles, and the couple rented a house. In 1928, they built a house

29. Okihiro, *Cane Fires*, pp. 45–53.
30. Edward D. Beechert, *Working in Hawaii: A Labor History* (Honolulu: University of Hawaii Press, 1985), pp. 192–95.
31. Leonard Broom and John I. Kitsuse, *The Managed Casualty: The Japanese-American Family in World War II* (Berkeley and Los Angeles: University of California Press, 1973), p. 78.

in a White, middle-class, residential section of the city, "and when the family first moved into the neighborhood, they encountered veiled antagonism. One family on the block was openly hostile, and they are suspected of having put up a sign reading 'No Japs Wanted' and of strewing nails on the driveway," reported the interviewer. But most neighbors were tolerant, if not cordial, and the family stayed in their seven-room home until World War II.[32]

Mary Oyama Mittwer recalled that Los Angeles's Little Tokyo during the 1930s was "a busy, buzzing little place as the center of California's Southland for *Issei* and their *Nisei* offspring." "As a whole," she wrote, "*Nisei* in Los Angeles lived in fairly new, better and more comfortable homes than did their counterparts in Northern California. Their homes were *hakujin* (white people) style, with trees, lawns and ample back yards rather than being in old, decrepit buildings in the shabby part of town as in other Japanese centers. This was because in the 1930's Los Angeles was still a wide-spaced, green-lawn town, horizontal, and with lots of room for expansion. The Japanese also were beginning to acquire cars, one to a family, to meet the transportation needs of the sprawling city."[33]

Although the exteriors of the houses were generally predetermined by their European American builders, the interiors and the surrounding gardens could be and were personalized by their Japanese American inhabitants. Robert Yasui remembered helping his father tend the plantation camp's large community *furo*, or bath, in Hawaii. "As kids we helped my father run the furos which were heated with firewood," he recalled. "Every Saturday and Sunday, we had to saw long keawe [a hardwood tree] stumps for the week. Later, we switched to charcoal. The furo was open from 2 to 8 P.M. on a first come, first served basis. The cost was 35 cents for single people and 60 cents for a family. The furo was one big, huge bathtub, like a shallow swimming pool, which was partitioned to separate men from women, but the kids swam back and forth under it." Yasui explained: "To the Japanese a hot bath was a daily must because being clean was very important. Sitting on stools, people first scrubbed themselves thoroughly before stepping into the steaming hot water to relax." Bernice Hirai described her childhood memories of *furo* bathing as "Such splashy, noisy laughter!"[34]

"The bath house was divided into two rooms, one for men and one for women,

32. Ibid., pp. 105, 110.
33. Bill Hosokawa, *Nisei: The Quiet Americans* (New York: William Morrow, 1969), pp. 164–65.
34. Hazama and Komeiji, *Okage Sama De*, pp. 55, 58.

just as in Japan," said Tsuneki Kagawa, proprietor of a bathhouse in Portland. "The tub for men had room for seven or eight persons, while the one for women could accommodate four or five. In addition, each room had two showers. I put hair tonic, bath powder, a fan, and pots of flowers in the rooms and kept the rooms clean." Kagawa opened his bathhouse at noon and closed at about midnight. "Every weekday I had about fifteen men and ten women," he reported. "But on weekends about thirty men and twenty women with children came to my bath. The little Nisei amused themselves in the big bathroom, playing about."[35]

Family gardens rendered ordinary house structures unique, bearing the stamp of their occupants, and for many they provided a great source of pleasure and, often, food. Grace Shibata described her mother, Take Eto, in her California garden during the 1930s. "At age forty-three, Mother is slightly under one hundred pounds, energetic and fit. The soft-spoken Issei woman stands five feet tall, looking relaxed in her print cotton dress, which falls loosely to her ankles. Under her wide-brimmed straw hat, her straight, black hair is pulled softly back to a bun. . . . She is enjoying one of her favorite pastimes, gardening. Early mornings and late afternoons," Shibata wrote, "she tends her snapdragons, sweet peas, dahlias and myriad other flowers which bloom in their season. At the far end of the garden are several golden sunflowers, full of dark seeds, towering perhaps eight feet tall. A chubby yellow and black bumblebee searches for nectar on a dahlia, and two small white butterflies flutter silently, dipping left and then right. The serenity of the garden befits Mother's character."[36]

In Hawaii, an architect described the plantation homes built after the 1909 and 1920 strikes on Oahu. "Many of the architectural features in housing for the masses in modern Hawai'i can be traced to the influence of plantation houses which were simple, low cost, box-like residences which made efficient uses of available materials. . . . The single-wall houses of pine and redwood were remarkably efficient, economical and appropriate to Hawai'i's mild climate. Single walls provided added sanitary benefit of eliminating cavities where disease carrying vermin could live."[37]

Having spent my childhood in one of those "simple, low cost, box-like residences," I can attest to their appropriateness and economy. But I also remember how the corrugated tin roofs acted like radiators that transmitted the sun's heat into

35. Ito, *Issei*, pp. 861–62.

36. Mei T. Nakano, *Japanese Ameican Women: Three Generations, 1890–1990* (Berkeley: Mina Press, 1990), pp. 75–76.

37. Hazama and Komeiji, *Okage Sama De*, pp. 90–91.

the house, how the sound of each raindrop was amplified by the metal sheets into a deafening roar during a downpour, how the small windows barely let in the cooling mountain breezes, how rats and birds scurried across our roof and cockroaches as big as giant dates thrived in virtually every nook and cranny of the house, and how termites ate out the insides of the walls and floors, making them paper thin on the outside and allowing us to peel the skin away to reveal cavities filled with their waste matter. Lying on my bed as a boy, I looked up and imagined how the weight of decaying bodies made the ceiling sag, and how their moisture seeped through, stained, and slowly spread across the ceiling's whiteness.

Most people planted mango trees in their yards for shade but also for the delicious fruit, which was eaten raw or soaked in a mixture of soy sauce, sugar, salt, and pepper and called "shoyu mango." My father cut the skinned mango into strips and laid them out on newspapers spread on our garage roof to dry in the sun. He then cooked the dehydrated mango in a delicious sweet-and-sour sauce, learned from the Chinese, and made preserved mango, called "mango seed." Choki Oshiro, reflecting on his retirement, described himself as an "old man in Hawaii, which is a small state, but I have fruit trees, such as orange, avocado, banana and fig, in my own yard. In mango season," he continued, "my grandchildren come over and eat our mangoes, which is a great joy to me. Watering, picking up fallen leaves—such a daily routine is enjoyable. I am glad I can do it, because such yard work is ideal for keeping healthy."[38]

At the back of our plantation home, we had papaya, banana, mountain apple, macadamia nut, and avocado trees, and several raised beds of vegetables that featured green onions, daikon (a kind of radish), Chinese mustard, Filipino beans, and other Asian vegetables, along with string beans, carrots, and beets. Some of the clearest pictures that remain in my mind from childhood include my father wearing only Bermuda shorts, his dark brown bare back glistening with perspiration in the sun, wielding his cane knife as he bunched the branches and leaves from the mango tree, which needed an annual pruning because it grew so quickly. And the bent figure of my grandmother, head covered with a kerchief to shield her from the sun, hunched over her rows of green onions is still vivid in my mind's eye. They tended their garden well. Behind the vegetable gardens was the chicken coop, built

38. Ethnic Studies, *Uchinanchu*, p. 421.

above the ground to protect the chickens from dogs and the mongoose that lived in the cane fields across the road. Our yard was a veritable supermarket, providing us with fruits, vegetables, eggs, and meat. Whenever we ate chicken, my grandmother boiled a tub of water over an outdoor wood fire, thoroughly immersed the fowl in the hot water, and carefully plucked all of the feathers thus loosened by the soaking. Chicken dinners were a major project.

During the Great Depression, having chicken for dinner was a great luxury. In Seattle, people sang the "Doughnut Song":

> In the morning I had doughnuts and coffee.
> At noon I had coffee and doughnuts.
> In the evening I had doughnuts and coffee.[39]

"It was the Depression time, and the price of grapes was pretty bad," recalled Hanayo Inouye of California. "Women were getting paid one fifty a day for ten hours of work. For men it was two dollars a day. It was especially hard in those days for those who were in business for themselves. For instance, a family that used to run a vegetable store said they had not had meals for days because of the high cost of rice." To help alleviate some of the poverty within the Japanese American community, Inouye and others who could afford it brought a cup of rice and canned goods to the Japanese-language school for distribution to needy families once a week.[40]

"We did not go hungry, but it was very difficult," said Wataru Ishisaka. "It was the same with everybody else. As you know, the Japanese are a proud people, and they will not accept charity from anyone. But we knew some people who were suffering greatly. They had lots of children and lived in shacks under the levee by the river. We used to take a sack of rice and other food and roll the goods down the levee. Then, you see, they wouldn't know who the donor was, and they could accept the food," Ishisaka explained. "The Depression time was a very difficult time for all people. In Sacramento many people were picking things out of garbage cans." The Japanese Association, he recalled, organized a relief effort that distributed food to the needy at night to avoid embarrassing them.[41]

In Washington, A. Ichida, a member of the Salvation Army, collected vegetables from farmers and stale bread from Japanese bakeries and "secretly delivered them

39. Ito, *Issei*, p. 849.
40. Sarasohn, *Issei*, p. 147.
41. Ibid., p. 148.

to people whose lives were difficult," reported Uhachi Tamesa. "Also he frequently took those who had nothing to eat to the Salvation Army and gave them meals. Some who were assisted by him were deeply moved by his love and experienced a rebirth, giving up gambling and such." Ichida worked among Seattle's poor until 1940. "Because of the Depression," he explained, "farmers in the outlying districts just left their vegetables piled up in the fields. I got them and made pickles out of them and used them all winter. Also, canned and salted salmon, rice and *miso* were donated, and more than twenty families were able to survive on these donations." [42]

Another benefactor, Gentaro Kodashiro, was called by Juhei Kono "The Saint of Northern California." Kodashiro, according to Kono, once owned about ninety acres of orchard land near Vacaville. The Depression put an end to his farm, and so he sold all of his land and used the money for various causes. "He gave to the poor in a very quiet way; so we don't know the extent of what he did," said Kono. "The reason I know of him is that in 1932 I was in charge of churches in the Vacaville and Palo Alto areas and met some of those people who knew about him. It was seventeen miles between his house and the church. On Saturdays he left his house on foot and visited Japanese homes on the way. He would leave food for those who were especially poor. He used to walk the seventeen miles, which took him two days. On Sunday he would attend church services and then walk back home." Kono continued: "During the night he would leave several pounds of rice at the doorstep of a needy Japanese family and disappear into the night. Nobody knew who gave them those things. Much later they found out it was Mr. Kodashiro." [43]

Tsuru Yamauchi described her plight in Honolulu during the Depression. "At that time I was really poor, very poor," she said. "I did not have a telephone at home. Besides, I had many children." She managed by working as a maid for Whites, who told her: "Clean our rooms. You can rest your children on our beds while you clean." "I would bring the babies along with me and lay them on the extra beds," Yamauchi remembered. "There were no babysitters then. The couple would both work so nobody was home. That kind of place would pay only a little money, but there was a lot of work doing that kind of thing." She also washed and ironed other peoples' clothes in her home, worked for three years at the Libby pineapple cannery during the harvest season for fifteen and then thirty cents an hour, and cleaned and cut fish

42. Ito, *Issei*, pp. 853, 854.
43. Sarasohn, *Issei*, p. 146.

at a tuna cannery. "I hated the smell," recalled Yamauchi. "It smelled so bad that I could not walk in front of people. But if I didn't do the work, I wouldn't be able to support my children." She explained, "This was the time of the depression and the kind of life our family had was difficult."[44]

Prohibition posed a minor irritant to some, who brewed their own, illegal liquor. "During prohibition days," Grace Shibata wrote, "Mother made *sake* for Father who liked to have a drink with dinner. She mixed *koji* (fermented rice) with cooked rice and water in a ten-gallon crock and stirred it periodically for several weeks while it fermented. It was tightly covered and, as the days passed, it started to bubble and foam. She poured this concoction into a clean linen sack which had been placed in a square wooden box, v-shaped at the bottom. With a weight on the sack, there came the drip, drip, drip of *sake* in the jug below."[45]

In Hawaii, Tokusuke Oshiro told about how Shiroma, his neighbor, brewed *okole-hao* (liquor made from *ti* root) and stored it in his room. The police raided Shiroma's operation and discovered where the liquor was stored. Oshiro was named as an accomplice but was offered leniency if he testified against Shiroma. Scared and concerned about his wife, who had just had a baby, Oshiro agreed to serve as a witness for the prosecution.[46] Oshiro's story reminded me of my grandmother, who distilled *sake* for my grandfather and who, according to my mother, bribed the local police but had her still smashed by federal agents in a raid. I wonder if my grandmother, a slight and innocent woman, even knew about Prohibition or understood the risk she took for my grandfather's drunken pleasure, which sometimes ended in curses and abuse.

Japanese migrants created a vital and coherent culture by trimming and altering their clothing, food, and houses and by striving to maintain aspects of their language, religion, kinship, and art. But the same processes that modified life's physical necessities worked upon the patterns of their behavior. Christian minister Takie Okumura arrived in Hawaii in 1894 to find a Japanese community that had many needs. "Not long after my arrival in Hawaii," he wrote, "I saw a little Japanese girl standing alone at the door of the church. Thinking that she might be lonely, I tapped her on the shoulder and inquired if she had come with her mother. She replied in a peculiar mixture of different languages, 'Me mama hanahana yo konani.' "

44. Ethnic Studies, *Uchinanchu*, pp. 500–503.
45. Nakano, *Japanese American Women*, p. 84.
46. Ethnic Studies, *Uchinanchu*, p. 385.

The minister could not understand her but was later told that "me mama" was "pidgin" English for "my mother," "hanahana" was Hawaiian for "work," and "yokonai" was Japanese for "cannot come." That mixture of languages among the second generation was widespread, and the inability of the *nisei* to speak "correct" Japanese distressed Okumura. "I felt keenly the need of establishing a school," he remembered.[47] Thus, on April 6, 1896, he opened the first Japanese-language school in Hawaii; soon language schools were built in virtually every community, from plantation camps to Honolulu, from California farm clusters to cities and towns.

The mixing of languages, however, was not confined to the second generation and might not have been a problem for the Japanese. Finding themselves among a diversity of groups and languages, Japanese plantation workers, like their fellow laborers, sought to learn and communicate in a common language. That necessity also derived from the bosses, who used pidgin English as a language of command. Choki Oshiro recalled learning "proper" pidgin English. He heard a fellow worker say that the time was "happa tsurii," which combined the Hawaiian "happa," "half," with the Japanized "tsurii" for the English "three." Thinking he could apply those numbers in other situations, he answered that he had cut "happa tsurii" bales of *pulapula*, or seed cane. His fellow worker laughed and corrected Oshiro by telling him that he should have answered "tsurii no hafu baiki," or "three and a half bags."[48]

In truth, linguistic syncretism was but a single aspect of a universe of associations and conjunctions. "My home life was a queer mixture of the Occident and the Orient," wrote *nisei* Aiji Tashiro in 1934. "I sat down to American breakfasts and Japanese lunches. My palate developed a fondness for rice along with corned beef and cabbage. I became equally adept with knife and fork and with chopsticks. I said grace at mealtimes in Japanese, and recited the Lord's prayer at night in English. I hung my stocking over the fireplace at Christmas, and toasted *mochi* at Japanese New Year. . . . I was spoken to by both parents in Japanese or in English. I answered in whichever was convenient or in a curious mixture of both."[49]

Growing up, the "queerness" of those syntheses never occurred to me. I thought my grandmother spoke to me in Japanese when she laced her sentences with words like *pau* (finish, end), *pilau* (dirty), and *poho* (waste) all derived from Hawaiian. And I thought I spoke English when I told her, "I no like wear no puka pants." I

47. Takie Okumura, *Seventy Years of Divine Blessings* (Honolulu: n.p., 1939), pp. 35–36.
48. Ethnic Studies, *Uchinanchu*, p. 415.
49. Hosokawa, *Nisei*, p. 173.

never thought it odd that my grandparents spoke to me in pidgin Japanese, and I responded in pidgin English. It seemed natural to me. Our combinations only appeared "queer" when "pure"-Japanese speakers insisted that my grandmother's Japanese was archaic or contaminated, and when "proper" English-speaking teachers in school hit my knuckles with their rulers, insisting that I forsake my pidgin tongue. "Only ignorant fools speak that way," they told me.

"Those adolescent years," recalled *nisei* Yori Wada, reminiscing about California in the 1930s, "were times to read the Tarzan books by Edgar Rice Burroughs and the cowboy westerns by Zane Grey—to learn at the Japanese Language School of Yoshitsune and Benkei, of the Heike-Genji warfare, of the Ako Roshi no Adauchi, of the Soga Kyodai." Cowboys and samurai roamed his mental landscape, said Wada, as seamlessly as dances for the dead (*obon*) and baseball and basketball games occupied his summer nights. Mischief also was a part of growing up, like stealing watermelons from "the carefully tended patch of an Issei farmer" or, on Halloween night, overturning outhouses.[50]

I am inclined to believe that most *nisei* children grew up loving and respecting their *issei* parents, despite the times in which they came of age—the "Americanizing" 1920s and 1930s. Americanization, the *nisei* were told, explicitly and implicitly by European Americans and some *issei*, demanded that they forsake the culture and language of their parents and adopt the conventions of the dominant group. Becoming American meant Anglo-conformity even if it resulted in a repudiation of one's self and parents. The *issei*, the Americanizers contended, were "Japanesy," old-fashioned and old-country, embodiments of the past; the *nisei*, in contrast, represented the future. Interracial misunderstanding and criticisms against the Japanese were the fault of the first generation, argued Takie Okumura, a Christian minister and leading Americanizer, who contended that "what the Hawaiian-born ought to do is to ignore the parents and adult Japanese and lead the young people in removing all the forces which retard their development as American citizens, and prove that they are good and loyal American citizens."[51]

Yori Wada wrote fondly of his mother, a picture bride from Fukuoka-ken, who "ran a small confectionery store selling *senbei* and *arare* and ice cream and sodas." Despite an apparent cultural distance between her and her children, Wada's mother

50. Yori Wada, "Growing up in Central California," *Amerasia Journal* 13, no. 2 (1986–87): 7, 8.
51. Okihiro, *Cane Fires*, p. 147.

communicated her desires to them. "She was a strong woman who rarely showed tenderness or gentleness to her children," Wada remembered. "But we knew, deep down in our hearts, that she cared very much for us and that she nursed the precious dream that her children would know a more comfortable life than hers. I do not recall ever being hugged as a child by my mother, but I knew of and received her abiding love. Coming home late at night after playing a high school light-weight basketball game in a distant town, I could count on her waiting up, with *ochazuke* and *takuwan* and some dried fish ready to serve."[52]

My mother, Alice Shizue Kakazu, dropped out of elementary school, despite her keen desire for an education, to help her mother and father rear her younger siblings and earn some income for the family that swelled to six sisters and five brothers. She was forced out of necessity into a lifetime of labor. But she and her sisters were also fun-loving teenagers, who grooved to Japanese and jazz and swing music, sang as a trio on Japanese radio, and hung out with the gang, both girls and boys. She belonged to the "in" crowd and had a boyfriend who had a car—the symbol of mobility and status—when my father came into her life. My father, Tetsuo Okihiro, was reared and educated in Japan; he was a Japan-*toso*, a *bobora*-head, an old-fashioned, Japanesy guy from the "out" crowd. But my father knew how to ingratiate himself with my mother's parents, whom he knew to be the lever that moved my mother. He brought gifts to them, milk and custard pie, and he helped them around the house, repairing their chicken coop and repainting their roof. And when he was ready to ask for my mother's hand in marriage, he sent a go-between to her parents and not to my mother. Of course, my grandparents thought fondly of my father and urged my mother to marry him. My mother was torn between her personal feelings and her filial respect for her parents, and after much agonizing, she agreed to the proposal. I know that my mother's suppression of romantic love and individualism was a manifestation of women's subordination, but I also believe that her remarkable acquiescence to her *issei* parents sprang from her *nisei* love for them, Americanizers notwithstanding.

But Japanese culture and *issei* parents constituted impediments in the lives of some *nisei*, who saw them as pathetic, even contemptible figures, and sought to distance themselves from the identity dualities they were accused of having created.

52. Wada, "Growing Up," p. 4.

Aiji Tashiro described a class of Japanese he called "Typs" for "typical Jap." "A 'Typ,'" he wrote, "usually needed a haircut or had too obviously just had one. . . . His father ran a grocery store; his sisters finished high school and worked in a market. The 'Typ' was enviably proficient in math and in art; totally lacking in the finer points of social grace. His clothes were incongruous and misfit. He either slunk timidly in the society of Americans or assumed a defiant, truculent air. He was impervious to self-consciousness, if the latter class, and persisted in jabbering loudly in Japanese in the presence of Americans. All 'Typs' cliqued together in school and out. The timid kind went on to college and became Phi Beta Kappas and 'Doctors.' The brazen variety became the denizens of pool halls and street corners. I decided that I was not a 'Typ.'"[53]

In 1939, a twenty-three-year-old *nisei* described his generation. On one extreme, he observed, there were "a large number" of *nisei* who "are, or try to be, intensely 'American.' They have adopted American conventions with a vengeance . . . some are ashamed of their parents' culture, and sometimes even of them as persons. . . . But their faces remain Japanese; and I have been told that some in this 'Americanized' element suffer occasionally before the mirrors in the privacy of their room, for their standards of facial and bodily characteristics also are 'American' or Caucasian." On the other extreme, there were "much smaller numbers" of *nisei* who "tend or pretend to accept their parents' old-country tradition. Many do not differ noticeably from their fathers and mothers; in fact, some strike one as almost more 'Japanesey' than their elders. . . . They are Orientals religiously." The majority, however, belonged to neither extreme, "but move, confused, between them; marginal people, neither here nor there, torn between two cultures, finding no function or satisfaction in either. They break away from parental control, but—well, they run into endless rows of *buts*, both in themselves and in their environment."[54]

Much of that confusion, I believe, can be traced to the two strands of anti-Japanese hostility that, on the one hand, sought to exclude the Japanese from American life because ostensibly they were unassimilable and, on the other, strived to include them but on the condition that they assimilate, or Anglo-conform. Both the "religiously Oriental" and "intensely American" *nisei* were responses to the excluders and includers. In the middle, Japanese American culture, hybridization, was

53. Hosokawa, *Nisei*, p. 173.
54. Louis Adamic, *From Many Lands* (New York: Harper & Brothers, 1939), pp. 221–23.

incongruous and indeed illegitimate within that cultural politics of polarities. "I am afraid that I cannot really attain objectivity by myself in any pure form," observed the twenty-three-year-old *nisei* cited earlier. "Nor can the rest of the Oriental second generation by itself. . . . You know how the cable cars groan and grind and jangle and rattle. All those discordant noises cut through any objectiveness I ever experienced." And he mused, "I rode uphill in a cable car. . . . I thought of my brother, of the artistic arrangement of fruits and vegetables in that store where he worked, of the fruits of the earth brought together and arranged in a pattern of beauty, harmony and color. . . . The car groaned and jangled."[55]

That uphill ride, that skepticism about ever achieving "a pattern of beauty, harmony and color" was bred by several lifetimes of experiences marred by the grind, the jangle, the rattle of discordant noises. "Once in Riverside I went into a barbershop, sat there, and started to read a newspaper," recalled Kengo Tajima. "While I was reading, the barber came and said, 'We don't serve you.' When I found out I wasn't wanted, I went out. I didn't know that Japanese were not wanted." "There was so much anti-Japanese feeling in those days!" exclaimed Choichi Nitta. "They called us 'Japs' and threw things at us. When I made a trip to Marysville to look for land, someone threw rocks. It took strong determination to decide to buy land and live here permanently." "The anti-Japanese movement by then had grown very important on the political level," explained Juhei Kono. "Because of the social climate, what is called the '*beika*-movement' [Americanization] became very popular among the Japanese."[56]

Heitaro Hikida recalled: "Not a single Japanese was allowed to enter the Alki Beach or the shore at Ballard" in Washington State. "Also, we were discriminated against in the high class movie houses and theaters. They would never refuse us entry outright, but would simply never sell us a first class seat. Instead they gave us balcony seats." Sentaro Tsuboi added: "I went to a theater on Third Avenue with my wife and friends. We were all led up to the second balcony with the Blacks." And Kane Mitsuoka remembered a day when his child was seven or eight years old. "He asked me for a quarter to go to the swimming pool with Douglas, a white boy who was our neighbor. So I gave him the money. He took his streetcar fare and swimming suit and went off gayly. But he soon came home depressed. To my question he

55. Ibid., pp. 233, 234.
56. Sarasohn, *Issei*, pp. 63, 64, 68.

145

answered, 'They let Douglas in, but not me. When I grow up, I'll build a huge pool and *never* let any whites in!' As a parent, I cried to hear it." The poet Fujio wrote:

> Because of my skin
> I hesitate near the pool.
> O, to just plunge in![57]

As "coloreds," the Chinese faced racism shaped by the European encounter with American Indians, Africans, and Latinos; and the Japanese, Koreans, Filipinos, and Asian Indians, as "Orientals," confronted racism molded by the European interaction with Chinese. "The racial discrimination in Washington, D.C. was terrible, especially towards black people," remembered Shokan Shima of his arrival in 1923. "If a black person encountered a white person in the street, the black person took off his hat and humbly passed by. It was a white-privileged society. . . . Because of prejudice, I had a real problem finding a place to rent. . . . Not one White . . . would rent me a room in their house. Wherever I saw a sign saying 'Room Available' or 'Room for Rent' and went to inquire, the White owner would come out, take one look and flatly refuse me, saying, 'You're Chinese. The room's not for rent.' If I replied, 'I'm not Chinese. I'm Japanese,' they would answer, 'It doesn't matter. I can't rent to you anyway.' I finally discovered a place where I could stay. It was the rather dirty upstairs of a Chinese laundry in the slum area."[58]

America's Japanese experienced racism, both personal and institutional, in various shades and forms. Like other minority groups, the Japanese, from Hawaii's plantations to Washington, D.C.'s streets, were the targets of hateful words, dung, and fists hurled at them, were circumscribed by housing and employment discrimination sanctioned as social practice, and faced legal impediments to citizenship and the guarantees of life, liberty, and property. The second generation, although U.S. citizens by birth, were the objects of special scrutiny as to their loyalty and were presented with the choice of abandoning their parents and culture to become "good and loyal American citizens" or remaining Japanese and facing ridicule and contempt. And despite acculturation, the *nisei* encountered racism that led to marginality, self-hatred, and stunted economic opportunities. "I am a fruitstand worker," a *nisei* wrote in 1937. "It is not a very attractive nor distinguished occupation. . . . I would

57. Ito, *Issei*, pp. 97–99.
58. Okinawa Club of America, comp., *History of the Okinawans in North America*, trans. Ben Kobashigawa (Los Angeles: UCLA Asian American Studies Center and The Okinawa Club of America, 1988), p. 473.

146

much rather it were doctor or lawyer . . . but my aspiration of developing into such [was] frustrated long ago. . . . I am only what I am, a professional carrot washer."[59]

But the Japanese also fought against racism; they were not simply its victims. "I had a bitter experience with exclusion," recalled Kyuichi Nagai. "When I was working at the roundhouse of Northern Pacific in Livingston, Montana, the whites made a fool of me, calling me 'Jap, Jap!' Since my judo skill was equivalent to black belt rank . . . , I buttocked them in front of me." Frank M. Tomori of Portland explained: "The reason why we practised judo so earnestly was to train our body and mind, but at the same time it was for purposes of self-defense against whites who called us 'Jap!'" "The tall white men frequently insulted the Japanese . . . by saying, 'Harro, Chary!' and roughing up our hair," remembered Chuji Sakata. "Since the Japanese were no match in such a situation, and also were in a minority, even the whites paid respect to those among the Japanese who were strong. I have achieved the seventh grade in judo training and am 5′5″ tall, and I was never insulted or excluded."[60]

"There was no one who wasn't whipped," said Chinzen Kinjo of life on one of Hawaii's sugar plantations. "Once when this luna whipped me by taking me for someone else, I was really mad," he recalled, "and all the anger which had hitherto been suppressed in me exploded and I challenged him with karate. Since this luna was a big man, a six-footer, it wasn't easy for me. But, finally, I threw him to the ground. . . . There was a big crowd surrounding us, some waving cane knives, shouting, 'Kinjo, go ahead, go ahead!' The others shouted 'Beat him up! Finish him!' I was at the point of jumping at him, risking my whole life in that one blow," confessed Chinzen. "Just at that moment, Big Luna came and calmed me down, saying, 'Wait, wait. I will fix everything all right.' Thus, the incident ended short of serious consequences. We wanted revenge even to the point of committing murder. You can understand how brutally the laborers of early years were treated."[61]

While some Japanese tried to take matters into their own hands, others sought remediation and redress through the courts. In July 1925, fifteen Japanese hired by the Pacific Spruce Lumber Company in Toledo, Oregon, were attacked by a mob of several hundred Whites, who charged behind an American flag, brandished weapons, and shouted "Drive out Japs!" "Lynch Japs!" The Japanese were rounded up, forced into a truck with their luggage, and driven out of the lumber camp.

59. Roger Daniels, *Concentration Camps: North America, Japanese in the United States and Canada during World War II* (Malabar, Fla.: Robert E. Krieger Publishing, 1981), p. 23.
60. Ito, *Issei*, p. 133.
61. Kimura, *Issei*, p. 50.

After the local police refused to arrest the rioters, the Japanese victims sued six of the mob's leaders for compensation for damages suffered in the attack. The court ordered the assailants to pay the $6,500 amount awarded the Japanese, and the six defendants promised to refrain from future anti-Japanese activity.[62]

Takao Ozawa landed in San Francisco in 1894, worked as a school boy, graduated from Berkeley High School, and attended the University of California, Berkeley, for three years. In 1906, he moved to Honolulu, where he worked for an American firm. In 1914, Ozawa applied for naturalization, pointing out in his legal brief that he neither drank nor smoked, did not play cards or gamble, did not associate with "improper persons," and was honest, industrious, and upright. "As far as my character is concerned," he wrote, "I am second to none." As his case moved through the court system, he attested to his allegiance by arguing that he had lived continuously within the United States for over twenty-eight years, married an American-educated woman, did not attend Japanese churches or language schools but studied only in American schools, sent his children to an American church and school, did not belong to any Japanese organizations, spoke mainly English at home, and "have steadily prepared to return the kindness which our Uncle Sam has extended to me." He was denied naturalization on the grounds of his race, at the lower courts and finally by the Supreme Court in 1922.[63]

Other legal challenges succeeded. During the early 1920s, Hawaii's government tried to control and diminish the existence and influence of Japanese-language schools. Eighty-seven language schools joined in a litigation, questioning the constitutionality of the government's action. The case was finally heard by the Supreme Court, which rendered its unanimous decision in 1927 that acknowledged the difficulty of "the Japanese problem" in Hawaii but sided with the petitioners because, the Court ruled, "the limitations of the Constitution must not be transcended." At a mass meeting celebrating the victory, Kinzaburo Makino, a leader in the struggle, called the legal challenge "the right of a people living in a free democracy to seek legal clarification regarding constitutionality of their laws," and he urged the Japanese to rear their children as "good Americans capable of understanding both the English and Japanese languages." The lesson of this effort, reminded Makino, was

62. Ito, *Issei*, pp. 214–15.
63. Ichioka, *Issei*, pp. 219–26.

148

that "we must never forget that we have to stand up for our rights as guaranteed under the Constitution."[64]

The collective struggle for equality also took place in America's fields and factories. Japanese workers organized themselves into unions to fight against labor exploitation and repression. On February 11, 1903, 500 Japanese and 200 Mexican sugar beet workers formed the Japanese-Mexican Labor Association (JMLA) and went on strike against the Western Agricultural Contracting Company. They called for higher wages, reduced commissions paid by workers to labor contractors, and an end to the monopoly held by designated stores. The strikers swelled to 1,200 members, or about 90 percent of the entire work force, by March. After a violent confrontation in which a Mexican worker was killed and two Japanese and two Mexicans were wounded, the union sat down with the contractors and negotiated a settlement. When the JMLA applied to the American Federation of Labor (AFL) for a charter, Samuel Gompers, AFL president, wrote that the charter would be granted only on the condition that "your union will under no circumstance accept membership of any Chinese or Japanese." The JMLA secretary, J. M. Lizarras, a Mexican, replied: "We would be false [to the Japanese] and to ourselves and to the cause of Unionism if we . . . accepted privileges for ourselves which are not accorded to them." And he pointedly declared that workers should unite "without regard to their color or race."[65]

For four months in 1909, 7,000 Japanese sugar plantation workers on the island of Oahu struck for higher wages and equality in the workplace, and in 1920, 8,300 Filipino and Japanese laborers walked off the job, calling for higher wages for men and women workers, an eight-hour day, an eight-week paid maternity leave for women, and improved health-care and recreational facilities for laborers. Despite the multiethnic, class-based nature of the strike, the planters portrayed it as a racial and national security threat, as "an attempt on the part of the Japanese to obtain control of the sugar industry" and as "a dark conspiracy to Japanize this American territory." A federal commission sent by Washington to investigate Hawaii's labor situation in the aftermath of the 1920 strike warned of the "menace of alien domination" and of its belief *"that the question of National Defense and the necessity to curtail the*

64. Okihiro, *Cane Fires*, pp. 153–55.
65. Ichioka, *Issei*, pp. 96–99.

domination of the alien Japanese in every phase of the Hawaiian life is more important than all the other problems combined." And military intelligence surveyed "the Japanese problem" both in Hawaii and in California and alleged that Japan directed Buddhist and Shinto priests, Japanese-language schoolteachers, Japanese newspaper owners and editors, "radical" labor leaders, and pliant workers to advance its imperial designs.

"One of the most important features about this strike as far as the American community is concerned," wrote the head of military intelligence in Hawaii about the 1920 strike, "was the methods used by the Japanese in carrying on the strike. These methods brought home to the Americans the fact that when the Japanese have decided upon a course of action they allow nothing in the world to stop them from gaining their objective."[66] The report alleged that Japan, aided by "hosts of aliens, of radicals, or pacifists and of renegades of every sort and description now rampant in the United States," used strikes to saddle the American economy and to weaken the national resolve to wage war, "even when war is necessary to preserve the vigor of our nationality." While the nation slumbered, Japan continued "her peaceful expansion and penetration and her active procreation" in America to achieve its object of dominance in the Pacific, and "with the assistance derived from the pressure of other Asiatic races having a foothold in the Americas, she will make it vastly harder for America to finally resist her aims."[67]

That sentiment echoed some of the most strident "yellow peril" rhetoric of White supremacists, social commentators, and fiction writers that gained currency during the late nineteenth century. In 1880, Pierton W. Dooner published a fictionalized account, called "deductive history" by its author, of the Chinese conquest of America entitled *Last Days of the Republic.* The book detailed how an "eminently peaceful, industrious and law-abiding" people migrated to America, gained control of California's industries with their cheap labor, won political office through the ballot box, and rose in armed insurrection whereby the "swarming horde" overwhelmed the "brave defenders." "Forever occupied and diverted by its factions and its politicians, in their local intrigues for the acquisition of political power," wrote Dooner, "the Ship of State sailed proudly on, too blinded by her preoccupation and too reliant in her strength to bestow a thought upon the perils of the sea. . . . Too

66. Okihiro, *Cane Fires*, pp. 67–76, 79, 95–97, 111, 113.
67. Ibid., pp. 108–11.

late! She was hurled, helpless and struggling, to ruin and annihilation; and as she sank, engulfed, she carried with her the prestige of a race."[68]

English historian Charles H. Pearson, writing thirteen years after Dooner and during the noonday of European expansion, foresaw a global struggle for supremacy between Whites and peoples of color, between the inhabitants of the Temperate Zone and those in the Tropics. Western imperialism would stir the slumbering masses of the tropical band, science and medicine would lengthen their lives and create a population explosion, and industry and technology would enable them to produce more efficiently for the world market. All of that will encourage their spread from the Tropics to the Temperate Zone—the White homeland—and will provide them with the means by which to challenge White overrule. Asians, according to Pearson, would marshal and lead the resurgent masses.[69]

The global and U.S. "yellow peril" themes of imperialism, migration, economic competition, and military conquest provided ample fuel for the fires that continued to sear the public imagination during the early twentieth century. British author Sax Rohmer created in 1913 an archetypal villain, Fu Manchu, "the yellow peril incarnate in one man," and thereby personified the hitherto abstract, impalpable, but all-pervasive evil that threatened the "white race." In thirteen novels, three short stories, and one novelette that appeared until 1959, Rohmer pitted British agent Sir Denis Nayland Smith against the mad genius in a monumental battle of wits, science, and supernatural forces, in which, gasped the novels' narrator, "the swamping of the White world by Yellow hordes might well be the price of our failure." Not insignificantly, Fu Manchu, a son of the Tropics, operated within the Chinatowns of the Temperate Zone and, as a leader of barbarian hordes, possessed the "giant intellect" of the West and the "cruel cunning of an entire Eastern race," having "a brow like Shakespeare and a face like Satan."[70]

A few months after the 1920 sugar plantation strike, the Bureau of Investigation, forerunner of the Federal Bureau of Investigation, described the "Japanese problem" as "almost unbelievable" in scope. Japan, the bureau's agent contended, was bent on a "program for world supremacy" and saw California as a dumping ground for its "constantly increasing surplus population." If the tide of immigration was not stemmed, warned the report, "the white race, in no long space of time, would

68. Pierton W. Dooner, *Last Days of the Republic* (San Francisco: Alta California Publishing, 1880), preface and chap. 5.

69. Richard Austin Thompson, *The Yellow Peril, 1890–1924* (New York: Arno Press, 1978), pp. 18–21.

70. William F. Wu, *The Yellow Peril: Chinese Americans in American Fiction, 1850–1940* (Hamden, Conn.: Archon Books, 1982), pp. 164–74.

be driven from the state and California eventually become a province of Japan . . . , further, that it would be only a question of time until the entire Pacific coast region would be controlled by the Japanese." Yet Japan's ultimate aim was not limited to California or the Pacific Coast but was global domination achieved through a race war. "It is the determined purpose of Japan," the report stated, "to amalgamate the entire colored races of the world against the Nordic or white race, with Japan at the head of the coalition, for the purpose of wrestling away the supremacy of the white race and placing such supremacy in the colored peoples under the dominion of Japan."[71]

To underscore the seriousness with which they treated those apparently "fantastic" scenarios, the intelligence community and military planners charted a course of action for dealing with Japanese Americans in preparation for the coming great conflict. In 1922, the Bureau of Investigation maintained a list of 157 Japanese, including merchants, Buddhist priests, Japanese-language school principals and teachers, laborers, Christian ministers, and others under the heading "Japanese Espionage—Hawaii." A year later, Hawaii's military drew up defensive plans for a war with Japan that included a declaration of martial law, the registration of all enemy aliens, the internment of those deemed security risks, and the placing of restrictions on labor, movement, and public information. Before the end of the decade, the military proposed to classify all Japanese, aliens and citizens alike, as enemy aliens, and its criterion for internment changed from an adjudged capacity for espionage to simply a position of leadership in the Japanese American community.[72] Bereft of leaders, the reasoning went, Hawaii's Japanese would be cowed, confused, and easily controlled.

During the 1930s, as America's Japanese struggled to survive during the Great Depression, brewed illegal *sake* and *okolehao* despite Prohibition, and distributed food to the needy in the darkness of night, the military and civilian intelligence agencies spread their surveillance network and refined their plans for containing the "Japanese problem." It was during those preparations that President Franklin D. Roosevelt wrote to the military's Joint Board chief in Washington on August 10, 1936: "Has the local Joint Planning Committee (Hawaii) any recommendation to make? One obvious thought occurs to me—that every Japanese citizen or non-citizen on the Island of Oahu who meets these Japanese ships or has any connection

71. Okihiro, *Cane Fires*, pp. 116–17.
72. Ibid., pp. 118, 124–25, 128.

with their officers or men should be secretly but definitely identified and his or her name placed on a special list of those who would be the first to be placed in a concentration camp in the event of trouble." The president's "obvious thought" had been prompted by an intelligence report from Hawaii that discussed Japanese espionage in the islands, the visits of Japanese naval vessels in Hawaiian ports, and the entertainment of their officers and men by local Japanese residents. After reading that report, the president had asked the Joint Board chief and acting navy secretary, "what arrangements and plans have been made relative to concentration camps in the Hawaiian Islands for dangerous or undesirable aliens or citizens in the event of national emergency."[73]

The acting secretary of war responded to Roosevelt's inquiry, explaining that the army had established a "Service Command," which linked the military with Territorial forces such as the National Guard, police, and other civilian organizations, for "the control of the civil population and the prevention of sabotage, of civil disturbances, or of local uprisings" of "potentially hostile Japanese." And the Joint Board reassured the president: "It is a routine matter for those responsible for military intelligence to maintain lists of suspects, who will normally be the first to be interned under the operation of the Joint Defense Plan, Hawaiian Theater, in the event of war." But it underscored the need for continued vigilance and recommended that the resources of government, besides those of the army and navy, be enjoined for a common effort against the perceived danger. Roosevelt thus formed a committee chaired by the war secretary and consisting of the attorney general and the secretaries of labor, navy, state, and treasury "to work out some practical solution to the problem" of interagency coordination in curbing the alleged Japanese threat.[74]

Mary Tsukamoto remembered encountering prejudice during the 1920s and 1930s where "everyone whispered, and you felt kind of ashamed and afraid, and it made you kind of tighten up your body." "I remember how we meekly walked around and we huddled together," she wrote of her high school days, "and very reluctantly responded to invitations to various activities." Her trepidation stemmed from the propaganda campaign of the Native Sons and Daughters of the Golden West, the American Legion and California Federation of Labor, and the Hearst and

73. Ibid., pp. 173–74.
74. Ibid., pp. 174–75.

McClatchy newspapers, who "claimed that the Japanese were going to own all of California, that we were going to take over the land. . . . Prejudice was deliberately manufactured," she noted, "and people had to work hard to create and stir it up. We were innocent victims, but we have to understand this background if we are to understand what happened when the war broke out."[75]

That background, America's Japanese would soon learn, extended far beyond their youthful tormenters in school, far beyond the yellow journalism and political rhetoric of interest groups, far beyond learned treatises and "deductive histories," far beyond the imaginations of writers and filmmakers who helped conjure up and popularize the specter of race war. "Placer County, where we lived," remembered Shig Doi, "was a hotbed of prejudice and discrimination. It was really a hotbed. Many rednecks, I guess they call them. Even when we were in elementary school we would always have fights. If somebody said, 'Why, you dirty Jap . . .' those were fighting words."[76] The white heat of anti-Japanese hatred, on the ground, was felt in the everyday lives of Japanese Americans. And the heat, that hatred, emanated from the highest levels of government among men rightly concerned about Japan's ferocious imperialism in Asia but wrongly believing, indeed leading, the racist discourse of White supremacy.

The last rays of the sun had cast the Sierras and valley floor into semidarkness when we came upon Manzanar's cemetery at the back of the camp. A lone obelisk dominated the ringed-off plot of ground hallowed by the sorrowful human dust that lay buried in that solitary spot. "Memorial to the Dead" read the simple inscription on the obelisk written in Japanese characters. Because many families did not have enough money to buy monuments to mark off the graves of their dead, approximately sixty volunteers from the Buddhist Young People's organization, under the direction of landscape supervisor R. F. Kado, erected the memorial in August 1943 to commemorate not only those who were buried there but also all of America's Japanese. "I built it for all the Japanese people and I built it to last a long, long time," Kado explained.[77] We found our way back to the car in total silence, and as we drove past Manzanar's gate and onto the highway that would take us back home, the remnants of the day's light disappeared and darkness descended.

75. John Tateishi, *And Justice for All: An Oral History of the Japanese American Detention Camps* (New York: Random House, 1984), p. 157.
76. Ibid., pp. 157–58.
77. Embrey, *Lost Years*, p. 1; and Armor and Wright, *Manzanar*, p. xv.

Dark

Pearl Harbor sits at the end of my street. Standing in front of my house on Pilikoa Street, I can look straight down toward Pearl Harbor and see the white memorial to the entombed crew of the USS *Arizona*. My mother told me stories of that December morning, when the Japanese fighters swept so low that she could see the pilots' faces as she ran for the cover of the mountains above our home. In our play, my friends and I swooped toward Pearl Harbor on our skatecars (homemade wooden cars with roller-skate wheels) as we sped down our street toward battleship row, and destiny. Long before World War II, U.S. naval intelligence officers had warned about the Japanese plantation homes built along Aiea's heights and about the splendid view they commanded of the harbor.

As a boy, I loved to fish in the forbidden waters of that naval base. Mullets, *papio*, and hammerhead sharks thrived in the brackish waters of Pearl. Once I watched with horror and fascination as the dorsal fin of a shark circled my bait, settled on it, and headed straight out toward Ford Island in the middle of the harbor with my line in tow, pulling until it snapped. Pearl Harbor was always within my sight and on my mind.

"I got up at 9:00 that morning," one of Hawaii's Japanese recalled of December 7, 1941. "Everyone in the household was out in the yard shouting and pointing towards the sky. I hurried downstairs to see what was the matter and my mother was the first to tell me that the 'Japs' had come. My reaction was one of complete disbelief. Even after I had looked towards the sky and had seen planes flying overhead and had heard the sound of cannon fire, I was still convinced that the army and navy were on maneuvers. I was so firm in my arguments that half of the family were ready to believe me until the radio announcer uttered the fatal words that we were being attacked by the 'Japs.' My mother kept running up and down the house, muttering a prayer as she did."[1]

"I do remember Pearl Harbor day," said Californian Mary Tsukamoto. "I was about twenty-seven, and we were in church. It was a December Sunday, so we were getting ready for our Christmas program. We were rehearsing and having Sunday School class, and I always played the piano for the adult Issei service. . . . But after the service started, my husband ran in. He had been home that day and heard on

1. Andrew W. Lind, *Hawaii's Japanese: An Experiment in Democracy* (Princeton: Princeton University Press, 1946), p. 102.

157

the radio. We just couldn't believe it, but he told us that Japan attacked Pearl Harbor. I remember how stunned we were. And suddenly the whole world turned dark. We started to speak in whispers . . . we immediately sensed something terrible was going to happen."[2]

In Honolulu, Tsuru Yamauchi remembered Pearl Harbor. "It was Sunday when it came," she said. "We were making *tofu*, and I was frying *age*. . . . The Aala Taxi man said, 'Hey, don't you folks know? War came!' We thought that he was only trying to scare us. I said, 'Huh?' and continued frying *age*. 'That's right!' he kept saying. From Beretania and King Streets, from both sides, cars kept passing by hurriedly. 'That's strange. Today something happened,' I was thinking. Then from Punchbowl, bombs were falling. 'We have to go home quickly!' . . . We could see smoke going up wildly from Pearl Harbor. 'What shall we do?' I thought. We were all afraid."[3]

"On December 7 I was already at work," said Miyo Senzaki in California. "Then the butcher motioned to me, 'Come over here, did you hear the radio?' I said, 'No, what happened?' 'Pearl Harbor just got bombed.' I said, 'What?' He said, 'I have a feeling there'll be people coming and antagonizing you, or they might say something to you, so just kind of stick close by, and signal me if anybody gets funny.'" Senzaki thought little of her friend's comment until a man came up and asked her, "'Are you a Jap or are you an American?' I said, 'I'm Japanese American,' so he said, 'All right then, you're okay, you're not just a Jap.' Then he walked away. Then I got scared." Later, she recalled, "the manager called us in back and gave us our paychecks and that was it. We were terminated, and then we got scared because we were thinking, gee, we got to go home." Senzaki eventually made it home. "The next day, Dad got scared and started to burn all the books, Japanese books," she continued. "He was panicking; he said to get everything out—all the records—and we just built a bonfire, busted everything, you know. When you panic and you don't know what's going to happen, I think you do these things without even thinking."[4]

"One morning—I think it was a Sunday—while I was working at Palama Shoe I heard, '*Pon! pon! Pon! pon!*' I was drinking coffee and I thought, 'Strange. Are they having military practice?'" remembered Seichin Nagayama, who was in Honolulu at the time. "At the corner of Liliha and Kuakini Streets, a bomb fell in the back of a cement plant. We felt like going to see what happened, the noise was so loud.

2. Tateishi, *And Justice for All*, p. 6.
3. Ethnic Studies, *Uchinanchu*, p. 505.
4. Tateishi, *And Justice for All*, pp. 100–101.

We found out that the war had started. The planes were flying overhead, and it was mass confusion. We worried about having enough to eat, having enough rice. I also worried about Palama Shoe. Here and there, people were getting arrested—the school was closed, the Buddhist priest was arrested, the teacher at school was arrested—that's all we heard about. At Palama Shoe I made shoes for the military. The FBI came checking at the store. They came to my house too. They looked at all my books and took the ones about Okinawa. I used to worry about going back and forth to the store."[5]

Twelve-year-old Donald Nakahata lived with his sister, mother and father, aunt, and grandfather in San Francisco. His father, who was a newspaperman and community leader, left for San Jose either on December 7 or 8 to help the Japanese Americans there. "And I walked him to the bus stop," remembered Nakahata. "We went down Pine Street down to Fillmore to the number 22 streetcar, and he took the 22 streetcar and went to the SP (Southern Pacific) and took the train to San Jose. And that was the last time I saw him." Nakahata's father was arrested shortly thereafter, held at a detention station in San Francisco, and sent to various camps reserved for the leaders of America's Japanese. "Dad was gone, and we just heard from him a little," said Nakahata. "We have a few letters from him. And you know, I have no feeling if I look at them now. He apparently suffered several more strokes in various camps. But I know he was in Fort Sill, Oklahoma, and Camp Livingston, Louisiana, and I think he died in Bismarck, North Dakota. It's really kind of sad if you think about it, that I don't know where he died."[6]

"When World War II began in 1941," recalled Chokame Hokama, "I as a Japanese felt very uneasy, since it was a war between America and Japan. I remember the blackout time—here in Lanai. We closed all the windows and made sure there was no light leaking through. The watchman would come around, and if he ever noticed any light coming through, we would be summoned and scolded." Japanese schoolteachers, a principal, a Buddhist priest, a Christian minister, and a Japanese *luna* were all summoned, questioned, and sent to Honolulu for confinement. As treasurer of the Japanese school, Hokama was called in for questioning. "There were many people who were called in before me and interrogated," he explained. "They had been asked anything and everything, they told me. And you couldn't possibly

5. Ethnic Studies, *Uchinanchu*, p. 479.
6. Tateishi, *And Justice for All*, pp. 32–35.

tell the authorities lies, as they had already investigated you thoroughly before summoning you. Listening to these people, I was quite worried. I couldn't predict what I would be asked. In the interrogation room they listened to me, then said, 'Oh, on a certain day, this thing happened—do you tell us lies?' They even went so far as to ask me which I preferred—Japan or America."[7]

Indeed, Japanese Americans had been studied, argued over, classified, and marked for removal and confinement decades before war came to America. By early 1941, the FBI maintained a list of over 2,000 Japanese on the mainland, including fishermen, farmers, businessmen, Buddhist and Shinto priests, Japanese-language schoolteachers, newspaper editors, travel agents, martial arts instructors, and community leaders, grouped in to A, B, and C categories that designated the supposed danger they posed.[8] The list resembled the 1922 version drawn up by the Bureau of Investigation of Hawaii's Japanese, in that they both sought to identify the leaders of Japanese America for the purpose of confining them in the event of war. That program of selective detention was designed to control the population as a whole by leaving them bereft of their leaders and fearful of a similar fate. "Fear of severe punishment," stated an army document in Hawaii, "is the greatest deterrent to commission of crime." And Hawaii's governor before the army's declaration of martial law on December 7, 1941, would later reflect upon the wartime measures: "Internment of all suspected enemy aliens," he declared, "was the only safe course to put the 'fear of god' in the hearts of those who would assist the enemy."[9] The poet Risuke Yasui attested to that fear among Hawaii's Japanese when he wrote on December 7:

> Intense anxiety,
> With rumors and false information,
> A day is now toward the end.[10]

While the smoke still rose from the wreckage of America's Pacific Fleet, arresting squads of FBI agents, military police, and local law enforcement officers knocked on the doors of persons listed on that team's index cards for apprehension in Hawaii. And during the evening of December 7, the FBI teletype crackled with the urgent message: "Immediately take into custody all Japanese who have been classified in A, B, and C categories in material previously transmitted to you. Take immediate

7. Ethnic Studies, *Uchinanchu*, pp. 460–62.
8. Bob Kumamoto, "The Search for Spies: American Counterintelligence and the Japanese American Community, 1931–1942," *Amerasia Journal* 6, no. 2 (1979): 45–75.
9. Okihiro, *Cane Fires*, pp. 211, 212.
10. Ibid., p. 212.

action and advise Bureau frequently as to exact identity of persons arrested. Persons taken into custody should be turned over to the nearest representative of the Immigration and Naturalization Service." By December 9, 1,291 Japanese, 865 Germans, and 147 Italians were in custody in Hawaii and on the U.S. mainland.[11]

One of those picked up by the arresting squads in Honolulu was newspaper publisher Yasutaro Soga. The events of December 7 filled him with apprehension and dread. Instead of putting on his usual kimono, Soga dressed in a suit and slipped on his shoes. In the evening, his eldest son, Shigeo, answered the knock at the door. "There were three, taller than six feet and young, military policemen," recalled Soga. "They told me to come to the immigration office. Without hesitation, I replied, 'surely' and went to my bedroom to wear my vest and coat." His wife accompanied him outside to the gate, and as he left, she whispered to him, "'Don't catch a cold.' I wanted to say something," he remembered, "but the voice couldn't come out."[12]

In his once familiar hometown, Soga lost all sense of direction as his captors sped through the blacked-out and deserted streets of Honolulu, stopping only to collect other "subversives" and to comply with the armed sentries who manned the various roadblocks in the city. When they arrived at the immigration station, the men were led into a dimly lit room where military police searched them and confiscated many of their personal possessions. Soga was half-carried upstairs in the dark by a soldier, who suddenly threw him into a room. "I didn't know how many people were kept in the room, but I couldn't find an inch [of] space for myself to sit down." He stumbled around in the disquieting darkness until a kind hand led him to the top of a bunk bed, where he sat listening to the muted voices in the room. Occasionally, within that lightless, spare space designed to dehumanize its inmates, someone would exclaim upon recognizing the voice of another in the room and thereby reestablish individuality, identity, and community.

With daybreak, Soga could discern the rows of triple-decked beds and bed mats on the floor and counted sixty-four "brothers," many of whom he knew, crowded into that single room. The men swapped arrest stories, Gikyo Kuchiba claiming to have been the first to be interned, at 3:00 P.M., and Tokue Takahashi recalling that he was collared while watching the Japanese attack with binoculars from his Alewa

11. Ibid., p. 210; and Kumamoto, "Search for Spies," p. 69.
12. These accounts of internment at Honolulu's immigration station and Sand Island are taken from Okihiro, *Cane Fires*, pp. 212–24.

Heights home. But the harsh realities of war and internment imposed themselves upon the stories and sometimes frail bodies and minds of those old friends.

Soga described the atmosphere at the immigration station as "bloodthirsty," where the attitudes of the guards were "rough" and where "things could have burst into bloodshed once a false step was taken." On the first morning, explained Soga, a young military policeman was obviously disdainful of his wards and ordered them around brusquely at the tip of his bayonet. "I was so furious," he remembered, "as if my blood started flowing backward. I almost threw my mess kit at him." Soga noticed a fellow Japanese staring at the guard with "a pale face due to his anger," but who restrained himself because "if we had expressed our feelings, we would have died . . . a dog's death from the thrust of his bayonet."

Suikei Furuya described how the men tried to help the elderly and sickly Miyozuchi Komeya by piling up bed mats on the floor for him to rest on. But a guard noticed the men's violation of a rule that apparently limited one bed mat to each man, and he rushed into the room and proceeded to pull Komeya off the mats while cursing him, "God damn you!" The men protested, but the soldier disregarded their appeals and dragged Komeya completely off the bedding and onto the hard floor.

When they were first brought to the immigration station, the guards searched Shin Yoshida and Zensuke Kurozawa at bayonet point and told them that they would be shot at dawn the next day. Unaware that the soldiers were simply "joking," playing mental games with them, the pair decided to kill the guard who brought them their food and then hang themselves. That evening, as they primed themselves to jump their tormentor, an old woman showed up carrying their meal. Much relieved, the men dropped their deadly intention.

The treatment accorded these men at the immigration station was purposefully brutal as if in recompense for Japan's devastating attack on Pearl Harbor. The men were not confined because they had aided and abetted the destruction of America's fleet. Their captors knew that. They were singled out for special treatment because they were leaders of Hawaii's Japanese and because the Japanese in America and the Japanese in Japan were one and the same, according to the racist doctrine of White supremacy. But racism was not entirely hysterical or without benefit and gain. The detention of Hawaii's Japanese leaders served to ensure the docility of the race, compel their loyalty, and coerce their labor toward the winning of the Pacific war, the contest between imperialist powers east and west.

The crowded sleeping quarters, unsanitary and stinking toilets, fixed bayonets, and morbid "jokes" were all punishments inflicted upon the ruling class of Hawaii's Japanese colony. They underscored the relationship between master and servant. There was a large room in the immigration station, wrote Soga, one that could have housed a mess hall for the men. But instead they were forced outside into the courtyard, where "we had to eat in the yard no matter how wet the ground was, or even when the rain started pouring during our meal," he noted. And the Japanese always ate after the German and Italian internees and used the dirtied mess kits of those Europeans, which had been carelessly rinsed in a single bucket of water. "I couldn't stand that because even these prisoners looked down on us," remembered Soga.

Many of the interned Japanese from outlying towns and the other islands were sent to Honolulu's immigration station. Kaetsu Furuya, a Japanese-language-school principal on Kauai, was apprehended on December 7 and taken to a military prison in Wailua. Iron bars marked off his cell, and an iron slab was his bed. He was issued two blankets for his bedding, and he had to call out for a one-gallon can that served as his toilet. The place was so infested with mosquitoes that "we all got swollen faces from mosquito bites," he said, and breakfast consisted of black coffee and cracker so hard that "it wouldn't break even if you bit it." He and his fellow internees had to endure those conditions for about two months, before they were shipped to Honolulu.

Jukichi Inouye, another Japanese-language-school principal, was also held, like Furuya, at Kauai's Wailua military prison. Inouye had been arrested on the morning of December 8 and first taken to the jail in Waimea, where the quarters were cramped, the toilet was a bucket, and "there was no place to hide." After three days, Inouye and nine others were put on a "dump truck," without explanation, and driven away. "We were wondering where they were going to execute us," recalled Inouye of the rumors rife among the internees. "Some thought the graveyard that we were nearing was going to be the place. But then we went by it without stopping." The men were instead taken to Wailua, where they were locked up with Furuya and seventy to eighty priests, language-school principals and teachers, and other community leaders of Kauai's Japanese.

In February 1942, Inouye, along with Furuya and others, was taken from Wailua prison to the port at Nawiliwili for transportation to Honolulu. Among the crowd of internees at Nawiliwili that day was Umeno Harada, the wife of Yoshio Harada of Niihau, who had befriended and assisted a downed Japanese pilot from the Pearl Harbor raid. Harada and the pilot, Shigenori Nishikaichi, both died during an escape attempt, and his wife was arrested and accused of being a spy. Umeno Harada was taken from Niihau to Kauai, away from her three young children, and placed in solitary confinement at the Waimea and later the Wailua jail. Armed guards watched her constantly, they questioned her frequently, and handcuffed her whenever she was moved from her cell to the interrogation room. In protest, she refused food for five days; a minister was summoned to restore her will to live.

Kaetsu Furuya noticed Harada at Nawiliwili port as they were about to be shipped to Honolulu. "At the time of departure," he recalled, "it was impossible to leave without pain and tears, especially in the case of Mrs. Harada, who had two or three young children, about five years old or younger." Umeno Harada would not have been able to say goodbye to her children had it not been for the compassion of a Korean American soldier, who escorted the children to their mother. That act of kindness, observed Furuya, held special meaning to Harada and other Japanese, because of Japan's brutal occupation of Korea and because of Japanese racialism that held that Koreans were inferior. "All of us who witnessed the incident cried," he said.

Myoshu Sasai, a Buddhist priest on the island of Hawaii, was taken into custody by a Hilo police officer and two soldiers the day after Pearl Harbor. Sasai knew the police officer well, whom he had counseled and befriended through a bumpy marriage. "They would have an argument, the husband and wife," Sasai explained, "and I would call them over and have a meal with them and make them shake hands." Now the officer took the priest away from his wife and young child to confinement at the Kilauea Military Camp. Throughout the night, buses emptied their loads, and by morning the camp held more than a hundred inmates. Sasai was shocked at the starkness of the camp—the barracks lined with beds and lockers, the gauntlet of soldiers that marked the path to the mess hall, and the outdoor toilets that required a guard escort every time an internee went to use them. Hishashi Fukuhara remembered an internee who tried to escape by climbing the fence. "They killed him," Fukuhara said of the soldiers, "they shot him dead."

Sasai and other internees from Hawaii were transferred to Honolulu in February. Their families were permitted to enter the camp barracks to bid them farewell, but recalled Sasai with sadness, "we really didn't have too much to say besides take care of yourselves and stay well. The talks were long, but that's what it boiled down to." Army trucks transported the men to Hilo Harbor, from whence they set sail for Oahu. "Normally the ocean is pleasant," observed Sasai of the voyage, "but in wartime, the ocean is scary. You don't know what is in it." At Honolulu's immigration station, the ubiquitous guards carried machine guns, noted Sasai, the bugle roused the internees every morning, and "even the food was bad. Pork and beans and sausage was the mainstay," he reported.

Honolulu's immigration station was the port of entry for many migrants from the nineteenth to early twentieth century, including some of the very men and women confined in it during World War II. Its walls might have still held my grandmother's fears, regrets, and hopes as she whispered in the dark, waiting for my grandfather to claim his bride. Indeed, the place must have been filled with the voices of the women, men, and children who had passed through its doors. During the war, the station served as a collecting point for many of Hawaii's internees.

Across the harbor, within clear view of the immigration station, was Sand Island, a flat, desolate piece of land that had at one time served as a place of quarantine for the thousands of migrants who landed in Hawaii. The government had sought to preserve the good health of its people by shielding them from the ravages of diseases brought in by passing ships. After Japan's attack, the government took over the health station on Sand Island and transformed it into a concentration camp for those it sought to quarantine from the rest of Hawaii's people.

The army selected Sand Island for a concentration camp because its facilities could be converted without much difficulty, it could be easily guarded, and it was close to the headquarters of Hawaii's military governor and the intelligence units that captured and supplied its inmates. The first group of internees were sent to Sand Island before the end of the first week of the war. Yasutaro Soga recalled being greeted by the camp commander, John G. Coughlin, who indicated that he considered the internees "prisoners of war," which drew Soga's retort: "His speech was agreeable to me, but I felt a doubt about the word 'POW.'" The group was then ushered into a room where they were stripped naked and searched, then herded outside in the rain and gathering darkness and ordered to erect the tents that would house them. "We were soaking wet from rain and perspiration," wrote Soga, "and finally we finished building tents about 9 o'clock at night." The first contingent was soon joined by another group, including the sickly Miyozuchi Komeya, who had fainted and had to be carried to his tent. Soga reported of their first day on Sand Island: "We all lay ourselves in makeshift beds in wet clothes that night."

Sand Island's terror worked on both the body and the mind. Strip searches were a common procedure designed to peel away the outer defenses of the self. When they were first introduced to the island, the internees were stripped naked and searched. When there was a violation of rules, such as when an inmate tried to commit suicide by slashing his wrists with a razor blade, the men were subjected to strip searches. An internee would later remember the indignity of those strip searches. "They stripped us down and even checked the anus," he exclaimed. "We were completely naked. Not even undershorts. They even checked our assholes."

The notion that one's body was not one's own was made obvious by the fact of detention, but it was underscored by the gratuitous acts of brutality that accompanied confinement. The day before New Year's Eve, remembered Soga, the camp commander called all of the male Japanese internees together to make an example of George Genji Otani, whom the men had chosen as their leader. Carl F. Eifler, the commander who had replaced Coughlin, said that Otani had been insolent to one of his soldiers, and for that, he sneered, Otani "should have been promptly shot to death." Instead, with "a threatening look," he ordered guards to take Otani to army headquarters at Fort Shafter, hold him in an isolation cell, and feed him only water and hard crackers for a week. On another occasion, an internee testified that guards with rifles lined the inmates up against a wall and threatened to shoot them if they disobeyed their orders. "With that threat," he added dryly, "there was no need to say anything more." And Soga noted that an internee risked being shot for failing to respond properly with the word "Prisoner" to a guard's command of "Halt!" "They ruled it our mistake to be shot if we didn't say it," he explained.

The camp's physical environment and the attitude of its keepers also stressed the unimportance of the inmates' well-being. "A dust wind kept blowing almost every day in December," reported Soga, "and the night air was shivering cold." When it rained, the camp flooded, the tents leaked, and the men's sleeping cots, set on the ground, frequently stood in huge pools of water. The internees' bedding, clothing, and supplies were perpetually damp from the rain and the humidity. Kokubo Takara caught a cold after being forced to stand in the rain, wrote Kaetsu Furuya. "The boss [Eifler] there made us, us men, really cry," he remembered. "It was February and it was rainy—the rain would come down from the mountains and this boss would make us stand in the rain, practically naked, in our undershirt and underpants." Takara received no medical care from the camp administrators for his cold and constipation, and "we had no medicine or means of helping him, so he died," lamented Furuya.

The mental anguish of survival was compounded by worries about the loved ones they were forced to leave behind. "In the beginning we were restless because we were incarcerated without any investigations," explained Furuya. "But, as the days went by, our nervousness was gone . . . and we began to desire to have investigations as soon as possible, for we were certain that we could go home as soon as the authority investigate our records. We had never done anything wrong in our lives." He added that those who spent their many years in Hawaii believing in the American dream, rearing their children to become "100 percent Americans," must have felt betrayed, and "some of them became neurotic and others became insane," he noted. "I suspected that unless we were mentally strong," wrote Soga, "some of us would begin to have nervous breakdown[s]. . . . We were insecure and impatient." He reported that a priest went insane, insisting that he was pregnant. "Our joyless days continued day after day," observed Soga. "In order to divert our feelings, smutty stories (sexual and obscene) were popular in every tent."

We have only fragmented accounts of the women internees on Sand Island, mainly from the perspectives of men. At least eighteen Japanese and about ten

German and Italian women were confined in that concentration camp. Eifler's wife served as matron for those women, and unlike her husband, she apparently treated her charges with care and compassion. The Japanese women internees were on Sand Island for the same reason that Japanese men were sent there—because they were community leaders, including professionals, language-school teachers, and Buddhist and Shinto priests, but also because they defied the military, like Umeno Harada and Tsuta Yamane, who defended her husband when he was apprehended. Unlike the men, who lived in racially segregated units, the women internees were integrated, though separated from the men.

Japanese women left behind at home had to cope with maintaining the children and households on their own. When Dan Nishikawa was taken away, Grace was left with a seven-year-old son, a frozen bank account, and unemployment, having been forced to leave her job. Without an income and with a son to support, Nishikawa sold all of her household furniture and appliances at greatly reduced prices for money to buy food, and she "gave away" their entire hothouse of nearly 500 orchid plants, some costing as much as $125 each, for $25. She eventually had to vacate her house because of financial exigency. Her health suffered from the strain of trying to cope. "I became very ill," she said. "I went from one doctor to another, but they say there's nothing wrong. It's just nerves. I couldn't eat . . . it lasted for how many weeks, I don't remember. Even if I didn't eat for a few days, I just didn't get hungry. It was just like morning sickness; when you look at the food, you just don't feel like eating."[13]

On February 17, 1942, two days before President Franklin D. Roosevelt signed the executive order that would remove all of the Japanese along the West Coast, 172 Sand Island internees were directed to collect their gear and were transported back across the harbor to the immigration station. There the "troublemakers" were told that they would be shipped to concentration camps on the mainland. Upon hearing this, wrote Soga, most "no longer cared about their future because they were in despair," and even the strongest willed among them broke down and cried. On the morning of February 20, military trucks, escorted by jeeps mounted with machine guns, sped the internees through the back gate of the immigration station, past the family members who had come to catch a glimpse of their men. The internees

13. Hazama and Komeiji, *Okage Sama De*, p. 138.

168

boarded the *Ulysses Grant*, where they were hustled below deck for the one-week voyage to Angel Island in San Francisco Bay.

"That morning, as usual, I woke up at six and prepared breakfast," remembered Kiyo Hirano, who lived in Sausalito, a town adjacent to Angel Island. "Around ten, a phone call came from a friend who told me in a hysterical voice, '*Taihen, taihen*; a terrible thing has happened! The Japanese planes are bombing Pearl Harbor! Hurry up and listen to the radio!'" Hirano turned on her radio and sat in shocked silence. "That whole day I spent speechless, seated in front of the radio. I will never forget that morning of December 7th, 1941." She recorded the reaction of some of her White neighbors. "Among those whites who had been our friends just a day before were those who turned into enemies, who fired us from our jobs, who yelled, '*Get out Japs,*' in front of our doors." Others, though, told her: "'We have nothing against you. What wrong have you committed? You have led law abiding lives and fulfilled the duties of a resident. How are you different from us?'"

The government's reaction seemed to agree with the former group of White neighbors, noted Hirano. "Then also began the suffering of all those of Japanese ancestry residing on the Pacific coast and I, too, became one of the *enemy aliens*," she wrote. "By that evening, policemen, searching for such things as shortwave radios, visited my home and conducted an investigation. Some of the leaders, priests, and other influential figures of not only the Japanese League but also of all organizations related to Japan were, without reason, forcefully arrested in their homes or their work places, or while walking the streets. They were not even given the opportunity to exchange farewells with their families."[14]

Take Uchida remembered the disruption of her life following Pearl Harbor. "My husband, Setsuzo, and I were picked up by the FBI early in the morning of December 8, 1941, in Idaho Falls because we were Japanese-language teachers and my husband was the secretary of the Japanese Association, an organization assisting Issei needing help in interpreting business and legal problems," she began. "We were taken to the Seattle Immigration office immediately. We were not given a chance to store our belongings or furniture—just enough time to finish breakfast." Her husband was sent from Seattle to Bismarck, North Dakota, and Uchida remained interned at Seattle until April 1942, when she was transferred to the Federal Women's

14. Kiyo Hirano, *Enemy Alien* (San Francisco: JAM Publications, 1983), pp. 3–4.

Penitentiary in Seagoville, Texas, where she joined Japanese internees, women and children, from Peru and Panama, and where they later met women detainees sent from Hawaii. "Most of the ladies were schoolteachers and the educated wives of influential businessmen engaged in business with Japan," Uchida explained.[15]

Yoshiaki Fukuda, a minister of the Konko church in San Francisco, was apprehended on December 7. The FBI's allegation that he and other leaders of the Konko faith were agents of Japan planted seeds of doubt about Fukuda in the mind of even his wife. "Although she never believed the reports," he wrote, "her faith in me was shaken at times by the belief, widespread at that time, that a spy would never reveal his identity, even to his wife or children." After ten days, the detained men were herded to the train depot, where they boarded a train under armed military guard. "Although we were not informed of our destination," he recalled, "it was rumored that we were heading for Missoula, Montana. There were many leaders of the Japanese community aboard our train. . . . The view outside was blocked by shades on the windows, and we were watched constantly by sentries with bayoneted rifles who stood on either end of the coach. The door to the lavatory was kept open in order to prevent our escape or suicide. A gloomy atmosphere prevailed on the train. Much of this was attributable to the fact that we had been forced to leave our families and jobs with little or no warning. In addition, there were fears that we were being taken to be executed."[16]

Those fears could not have arisen without some foundation. Hawaii's internees held similar fears. Their summary apprehension, the grim condition of their quarters, the ever-present armed guards, arbitrary punishments, and threats of immediate execution worked upon the minds of the internees. Similarly, on the mainland, some Japanese internees were treated with brutality by their captors, from harassment like being fed food made unpalatable with too much salt or pepper, to incarceration in solitary confinement, to periodic beatings, which, in one case, caused the internee's front teeth to be knocked out. Guards provoked and threatened with unsheathed bayonets and commonly used handcuffs to restrain the internees.[17] Those practices, whether widespread and condoned by the government's Alien Enemy Control Unit or not, clearly occurred, and word of the abuse spread quickly among the subject population.

15. Take Uchida, "An Issei Internee's Experiences," in *Japanese Americans: From Relocation to Redress*, rev. ed., edited by Roger Daniels, Sandra C. Taylor, and Harry H. L. Kitano (Seattle: University of Washington Press, 1991), p. 31.
16. Yoshiaki Fukuda, *My Six Years of Internment: An Issei's Struggle for Justice* (San Francisco: Konko Church of San Francisco, 1990), pp. 7–8.
17. Tetsuden Kashima, "American Mistreatment of Internees during World War II: Enemy Alien Japanese," in *Japanese Americans*, edited by Daniels et al., p. 54.

Fukuda recalled the tension on that train as it left San Francisco and headed north toward Oregon. Believing that Japanese must "conduct themselves with dignity because the honor of all Japanese was at stake," Fukuda played a game with his fellow internees that cheered everyone up but that also poked fun at the absurdity of their treatment. He contrived humorous puns that described some of the internees and the "crimes" for which they were being "sentenced" to confinement. Yahei Taoka, head of the San Francisco–based Nippon Yusen Line and on whose ship six passengers once died of food poisoning, was sentenced by Fukuda for "not conducting adequate services to console the souls of the deceased." And Sakutaro Nakano, who snored loudly during his sleep, was sentenced to pay for the crime of "disturbing the sleep of others by sounding like a growling lion," while Imai and Inouye, employees of companies that bought oil for Japan, were arrested for "selling oil all the time," which translated into colloquial Japanese also means "always goofing off." When Rikitaro Sato and Hirotaka Ichiyasu were sentenced for having violated the blackout because they had bald heads, "everyone went into convulsions of laughter," reported Fukuda. "In this way nearly everyone aboard our coach was 'sentenced,'" he wrote. "Everyone laughed at the 'sentences' pronounced, ceasing to be despondent over his fate."

But others, picked up along the way to Missoula, "were handcuffed and looked very meek, as if they were sheep on their way to be slaughtered," observed Fukuda. "Whenever one would pass by me, I would encourage him by saying, 'Don't be afraid. Keep your mind at ease.'" On December 29, the train pulled up to the concentration camp. "Those of us who shared the same coach had agreed that, as representatives of the Japanese people, we should conduct ourselves with dignity," recalled Fukuda. "We walked with heads held high between two rows of soldiers armed with rifles with fixed bayonets."

After interrogations that revealed how carefully each internee had been followed before the war, 378 men were selected for shipment to Fort Sill, Oklahoma. These, the internees believed, were those deemed the most recalcitrant by the hearing boards, and some felt honored to be numbered among this group, while others felt shame for not being included. But some of the 378, Fukuda reported with undisguised disappointment, acted in an undignified manner. "Fearing that they might face a firing squad," he wrote, "some who came to bid me farewell were weeping. They carried their personal belongings over their shoulders and walked between two columns of soldiers standing at ten foot intervals. The scene of men crying while being herded like sheep was shameful, for Japanese should not show such weakness of spirit." He added: "I thought that we should not behave cowardly even if we were confronted with death. However, I did not think we would be executed without reasonable justification even if we were interned."

Fukuda's embarrassment at not being included in the first group was mollified when he learned that he was among the next group of about eighty destined for Fort Sam Houston in San Antonio, Texas. At the farewell party, Fukuda told the thousand or so internees who remained behind: "I am proud that I am going to be transferred. This means that I am classified a 100 percent honorable Japanese. I am proud of being a Japanese man. We do not leave here like crying sheep but rather like proud lions. To those of you who are staying here, behave in such a manner at the hearings so that you will avoid internment and be allowed to rejoin your families. If you should be transferred, please join us, holding your head high as a Japanese."[18]

Not all the internees faced removal and detention with Fukuda's confidence. Forty-five-year-old Ichiro Shimoda, a gardener from Los Angeles, was taken from his family by the FBI on December 7. On the train to Missoula, he attempted suicide by biting off his tongue. The other internees restrained him by placing a piece of wood between his jaws. Shimoda, a companion reported, had been deeply concerned about his wife and family back in Los Angeles and was thus despondent. At Missoula, Shimoda tried to asphyxiate himself, and, transferred to Fort Sill in March 1942, he climbed the inner fence of the camp and was shot to death by a guard. According to the FBI report: "One Jap became mildly insane and was placed in the Fort Sill Army Hospital. [He] . . . attempted an escape on May 13, 1942 at 7:30 A.M. He climbed the first fence, ran down the runway between the fencing, one hundred feet and started to climb the second, when he was shot and killed by two shots, one entering the back of his head. The guard had given him several verbal warnings."[19]

Whatever became of Ichiro Shimoda's wife and family, I wonder, and who bears the blame for his senseless death, the execution of this "one mildly insane Jap"? And what about George Hoshida, who was wrenched away from his pregnant wife and

18. Fukuda, *My Six Years*, pp. 8–12.
19. Kashima, "American Mistreatment of Internees," pp. 53–54.

three young children in Hilo and transported to camps on the mainland? Left without an income, his wife was compelled to institutionalize their eldest daughter, who had been left paralyzed by an automobile accident. While in the bath unattended at that facility, the child drowned. Who is ultimately responsible for that tragedy, and who will attend to that grief? "Of course I heard it was best that she went," remembered Hoshida sadly, "but not like that. Not like that."[20]

Back home in Hawaii and on the mainland, the families of internees faced uncertainty and the cold backs of friends and neighbors, who were fearful of any connections with those who had been visited by the scourge. In Seattle, Christian minister Daisuke Kitagawa recalled visiting the families of those who had been interned. "In no time," he wrote, "the whole community was thoroughly panic-stricken; every male lived in anticipation of arrest by the FBI, and every household endured each day in fear and trembling. Most Japanese, including at least one clergyman, were so afraid of being marked by association with those who had been taken away that they hesitated to visit the wives and children of the victims. Much of that fear can be attributed to the rumors, rampant in the community," Kitagawa explained, "about the grounds for those arrests, about the treatment the detainees were getting, and about their probable imprisonment for the duration of the war. No rational explanation could set their minds at ease."[21]

So while the rest of the nation girded itself up for the war against fascism, for the preservation of democracy, for the cause of righting a wrong—to remember Pearl Harbor—America's Japanese were paralyzed by a fear that turned them inward, toward themselves, toward self-doubt and even self-hate. Although racism had worked its corrosive effects upon Japanese Americans for over seven decades, the immediate source of the poison was the people's own government, led by a president who had an "obvious thought" in 1936 of concentration camps for certain aliens and citizens, and by other leaders in the cabinet, the Congress, the courts, state and local governments, businesses, and the press.

But all of America's people were not convinced about the peril posed by their Japanese neighbors, especially during the first two months of the war. The *San Francisco Chronicle*, for example, a paper notable for its anti-Japanese rhetoric, having warned its readers of a "Japanese invasion" in February 1905, editorialized on De-

20. Okihiro, *Cane Fires*, p. 262.
21. Daisuke Kitagawa, *Issei and Nisei: The Internment Years* (New York: Seabury Press, 1967), p. 41.

173

cember 9, 1941: "The roundup of Japanese citizens in various parts of the country . . . is not a call for volunteer spy hunters to go into action. Neither is it a reason to lift an eyebrow at a Japanese, whether American-born or not. . . . There is no excuse to wound the sensibilities of any persons in America by showing suspicion or prejudice. That, if anything, is a help to fifth column spirit. An American-born Nazi would like nothing better than to set the dogs of prejudice on a first-class American Japanese."[22]

And various church groups, amid the apprehension of Japanese American leaders, cautioned against the urge for mean-spirited action. Two days after Pearl Harbor, the presidents of the Federal Council of the Churches of Christ in America, the Foreign Missions Conference of North America, and the Home Missions Council of North America issued a joint public statement. "Under the emotional strain of the moment," they wrote, "Americans will be tempted to express their resentment against the action of Japan's government by recriminations against the Japanese people who are in our midst. . . . Let us remember that many of these people are loyal, patriotic American citizens and that others, though Japanese subjects, have been utterly opposed to their nation's acts against our nation. It is incumbent upon us to demonstrate a discipline which, while carefully observing the precautions necessary to national safety, has no place for vindictiveness."[23]

Everett W. Thompson, a Christian minister, described how Whites tried to help Seattle's Japanese. "In a few cases," he wrote, "we were present when an arrest was made and were able to help as interpreters. In many more, we called at the home shortly afterward to reassure the family that such an arrest was not a disgrace and that we had all confidence in the integrity of the arrested man. Next, calls were made on the men themselves in the local jail, and even several hundred miles away at the camps where they were being kept. . . . Many pastors and church workers had a share in arranging bank accounts or guaranteeing people now under suspicion because the FBI had taken their husbands or fathers, or merely translating and interpreting in business arrangements."[24] Hatred had not trickled down to all of America's people.

Meanwhile, among some of Washington's elite, the process of ascertaining blame for the Pearl Harbor disaster was under way. Despite the conclusion of the army's

22. Quoted in Morton Grodzins, *Americans Betrayed: Politics and the Japanese Evacuation* (Chicago: University of Chicago Press, 1949), p. 380.
23. Toru Matsumoto, *Beyond Prejudice: A Story of the Church and Japanese Americans* (New York: Friendship Press, 1946), p. 10.
24. Ibid., pp. 10–12.

board of inquiry that there was "no single instance of sabotage" and "in no case was there any instance of misbehavior" based on army and naval intelligence and the FBI, Secretary of the Navy Frank Knox told the press in mid-December that Pearl Harbor resulted from "the most effective fifth column work that's come out of this war, except in Norway." In January, he asked the secretary of war to provide "information as to [the] practicability of concentration of local Japanese nationals . . . on some island other than Oahu," and the following month, during a cabinet meeting, he proposed the internment of all of Oahu's Japanese on the island of Molokai.[25]

The navy secretary was not alone in seeking blame outside his department. According to historian Roger Daniels, Roosevelt's cabinet, meeting on December 19, 1941, decided that all of Hawaii's *issei* should be interned on an island other than Oahu, and Secretary of War Henry L. Stimson shared Knox's concern about the "dangerous Japanese in Hawaii."[26] Stimson, his assistant John J. McCloy reported, had talked to the president on the afternoon of February 11, 1942, and had received instructions from Roosevelt to "go ahead and do anything you think necessary . . . if it involves citizens, we will take care of them too. He says there will probably be some repercussions, but it has got to be dictated by military necessity, but as he puts it, 'Be as reasonable as you can.'"[27] What McCloy was relaying to the army's Western Defense Command in San Francisco was the president's decision to place the fate of the Japanese living along the West Coast in the hands of the military. On February 19, 1942, Roosevelt indeed signed Executive Order 9066, which authorized the military to designate areas from which "any or all persons may be excluded" and to provide for such persons "transportation, food, shelter, and other accommodations as may be necessary . . . to accomplish the purpose of this order." Thus began the years of mass exile.

Hawaii's Muin Otokichi Ozaki wrote about the darkness that descended upon Japanese America.

> I bid farewell
> To the faces of my sleeping children
> As I am taken prisoner
> Into the cold night rain.[28]

25. Okihiro, *Cane Fires*, p. 228.
26. Daniels, *Concentration Camps*, p. 52.
27. Ibid., p. 65.
28. Published in a collection of *tanka* in Jiro Nakano and Kay Nakano, *Poets behind Barbed Wire* (Honolulu: Bamboo Ridge Press, 1983), p. 15.

To be sure, within the course of American history, other forced removals "into the cold night rain" come to mind. I recall President Andrew Jackson's particular antipathy toward American Indians and their expulsion during his administration in the 1830s from the American South. I remember the thousands of Choctaws, Creeks, Chickasaws, and Cherokees who walked and died along the Trail of Tears to the "Great American Desert," to settle on land deemed unfit for human habitation. I note that Chinese Americans were driven out of California's Humboldt County in 1885, and Asian Indians, from Bellingham, Washington, in 1907. And I call to mind the African Americans who were driven from their homes in Rosewood, Florida, in 1923 by a White mob that killed at least eight people and burned down every African-owned home, church, and business in the town. Executive Order 9066 did not begin government sanctioned or abetted forced removals.

For Japanese Americans during World War II, the expulsions began in Hawaii immediately after Japan's attack. Although not on the same scale as the mainland's mass removal, over 1,500 Japanese on Oahu were forcibly evicted from their homes. Japanese farmers adjacent to Pearl Harbor were given two days to pack up and leave but were allowed back to move their livestock and harvest their crops during daylight hours. According to a report, those farmers suffered "heavy losses," some "practically all of their life's savings," because of the eviction. In late December, military police ordered all of the Japanese living in the vicinity of Honolulu harbor and the railroad terminal to move out by morning or be shot. Hurried arrangements had to be made to dispose of furniture and other belongings, to care for the sick and elderly, and to secure lodging. Those without places to go found temporary shelter at Kaiulani School, but a year later some were still homeless.[29]

Five days before Executive Order 9066, the navy ordered about 500 families of Japanese on Terminal Island, California, to leave their homes within a month. The islanders, mainly fishermen and cannery workers, lived in small, wooden cottages that they rented from the canneries. "The houses were awful," according to Virginia Swanson, a Baptist missionary on the island. "The Baptist Church was the one beautiful building on the Island," she added, "a symbol of hope for the people." Despite their simple life-style, the islanders were watched with great suspicion by intelligence agents because fishermen knew the coastline and communicated by

29. Ibid., p. 237.

shortwave radio, and because the island was within the port of Los Angeles and adjacent to the Long Beach Naval Station. On December 7, many of the island's *issei* were apprehended and confined by the FBI in communitywide sweeps. Swanson recalled how "the families huddled together sorrowing and weeping" as the men were taken away.[30]

So in February, when the entire community of islanders were ordered to move, the action came as no surprise to the remaining Japanese. Still, the swiftness and rigidity with which the order was served appeared particularly brutal. On the afternoon of February 25, without warning, new notices were put up informing the islanders that they had until midnight February 27 to vacate their homes. "Near panic swept the community," wrote Bill Hosokawa, "particularly where the family head was in custody. Word spread quickly and human vultures in the guise of used-furniture dealers descended on the island. They drove up and down the streets in trucks offering $5 for a nearly new washing machine, $10 for refrigerators."[31] Frequently, the loss of possessions gained only after years of toil was not the principal hurt; what really mattered was the loss of equality, fair play, and human dignity that accompanied this mean-spirited uprooting. A *nisei* volunteer who helped the islanders pack and leave wrote: "The women cried awful. . . . Some of them smashed their stuff, broke it up, right before the buyers' eyes because they offered such ridiculous prices." And Virginia Swanson saw beautiful wedding tea sets lying in pieces on the floor.[32] But it seems to me that the women who denied the "human vultures" a part of their lives regained a measure of dignity with each set they threw to the ground.

The Japanese Church Federation arranged sleeping quarters in various churches and schools in the Los Angeles area for islanders who had nowhere else to go, and White ministers and church members — Baptists, Friends, Congregationalists — used their cars, borrowed trucks, and donated mattresses to help the devastated community.[33] Virginia Swanson described the scene on the island during those last desperate hours: "The volunteers with trucks worked all night. The people had to go, ready or not. Some had to be pulled forcibly from their homes. They were afraid they were going to be handed over to a firing squad. Why should they have believed me," she asked, "telling them to get into trucks with strangers?"

At the Forsyth School, one of the reception centers, Esther Rhoads marked the

30. Audrie Girdner and Anne Loftis, *The Great Betrayal: The Evacuation of the Japanese-Americans during World War II* (London: Macmillan, 1969), pp. 110–12.

31. Hosokawa, *Nisei*, p. 310.

32. Girdner and Loftis, *Great Betrayal*, pp. 112–13.

33. Matsumoto, *Beyond Prejudice*, pp. 17–18.

floor with chalk to designate the space for each family. "All afternoon trucks and Japanese kept coming," she later wrote. "They were tired and dazed as a result of the sudden exodus. . . . We have old men over seventy—retired fishermen . . . and we have little children—one baby a year old . . . practically no men between thirty-five and sixty-five, as they all are interned either in Montana or South Dakota. . . . I feel especially sorry for the old men," commented Rhoads. "Where are these people to go? There are many Japanese with young leaders able to face pioneer life, but those who have come to our hostels represent a group too old or too young to stand the rigors of beginning all over again."[34] Terminal Island was just the beginning of a massive dislocation.

In early March 1942, Lieutenant General John L. De Witt, head of the army's Western Defense Command and in charge of implementing Roosevelt's executive order, issued proclamations that divided up the command into a "prohibited zone," essentially the coast and a strip along the Mexican border, and a "restricted zone," a larger area contiguous to the former. The restrictions applied to Japanese, German, and Italian aliens and to "any person of Japanese Ancestry," who were encouraged to move inland away from the coastal zone. Several thousand, perhaps 2,000–9,000, Japanese tried unsuccessfully to "voluntarily" relocate to unrestricted areas. "Those who attempted to cross into the interior states ran into all kinds of trouble," a government report noted. "Some were turned back by armed posses at the border of Nevada; others were clapped into jail and held overnight by panicky local peace officers; nearly all had difficulty in buying gasoline; many were greeted by 'No Japs Wanted' signs on the main streets of interior communities; and a few were threatened, or felt that they were threatened, with possibilities of mob violence." The interior states declared their refusal to become California's "dumping ground."[35]

De Witt's first proclamations designated restricted zones, established a curfew for enemy aliens, and prohibited all Japanese from leaving parts of Washington, Oregon, California, and Arizona, where most of them lived, but they did not order any removals or confinement. On March 24, the general issued a "Civilian Exclusion Order" that differed from his earlier proclamations and became a model for all other exclusion orders that effected the complete removal of Japanese Americans

34. Girdner and Loftis, *Great Betrayal*, p. 113.
35. Daniels, *Concentration Camps*, pp. 83–84.

from the West Coast. The target of his first exclusion order was the several hundred Japanese who farmed on Bainbridge Island in Puget Sound, near Seattle and also at the approach to Bremerton Naval Yard. Soldiers dressed in battle fatigues tacked up posters, "Instructions to All Persons of Japanese Ancestry," on the island's utility poles, at the post office, and at the ferry landing. The Bainbridge Japanese, mostly berry and truck farmers, had six days to close their farms, settle their affairs, and pack their possessions.

Bill Hosokawa described the "raw, overcast day" of March 30. "Although the Japanese had been given less than a week in which to settle their affairs and pack," he wrote, "they began to gather at the assembly point long before the designated hour, each of the fifty-four families carrying only the meager items authorized by the Army—bedding, linens, toilet articles, extra clothing, enamel plates and eating utensils. All else, the possessions collected over a lifetime, had to be stored with friends, delivered to a government warehouse, sold or abandoned. Farms developed over decades were leased or simply left to be overgrown by weeds." Armed soldiers directed the people onto a ferryboat, from which they viewed, some for the last time, their island home.[36] In Seattle, the islanders boarded a train that took them to California. "What impressed me most was their silence," wrote Thomas R. Bodine of the Bainbridge Islanders as they boarded the train. "No one said anything. No one did anything."[37] The train creaked out of the station and headed south for Manzanar.

The leaders of Hawaii's Japanese, too, were destined for California. Before being whisked away from the immigration station, Kaetsu Furuya described how the 172 men, the flower of their generation, were treated. "We had to be stark naked . . . on the bed and then we had our nose, mouth, hands, feet . . . anus, genitals, everything was examined carefully and then we had numbers written on our bodies. In red ink. Mine was '13.'" I understand that Chinese coolies, before they left China for the Americas, were stripped naked and had letters that denoted their destinations painted on their chests, *C* for California, *P* for Peru, and *S* for the Sandwich Islands. Once on board the *Ulysses Grant*, the Japanese were confined below deck for the ten-day journey to San Francisco. According to one of the men, their guards

36. Hosokawa, *Nisei*, pp. 308–9.
37. Girdner and Loftis, *Great Betrayal*, p. 134.

179

instructed them in the use of life vests but locked the door to their hold. "What is the use of life jackets if our door is locked?" he asked. "Unless someone came to unlock the door first, our lives had to go with the life of the boat." [38]

Angel Island, the golden door for thousands of Asian migrants, served as a prisoner-of-war camp during World War II. Perhaps Hawaii's exiles stayed in the very barracks that had held lonely and homesick Chinese, Japanese, and Korean migrants. Some might have read the plaintive poems carved on the barracks walls by Chinese who waited for admittance into America. "We were kept naked," recalled Suikei Furuya of their arrival at Angel Island. "Then we dropped down on all fours and our anuses were checked." He added, "My first impression of the mainland was really bad." The men were herded onto a train that took them eastward to Camp McCoy, Wisconsin, crisscrossing the tracks that took the Bainbridge Islanders to Manzanar. There the internees received a potato and two slices of bread for lunch, and dumpling soup (the mainstay of many *issei* migrant workers) and two slices of bread for dinner. The men, Furuya reported, "were always hungry."

Throughout the spring and summer of 1942, Hawaii's internees were scattered across the American landscape like the pink flower petals of the shower tree in a sudden gust of island trade winds. Before the winds subsided in 1946, the traces of Hawaii's Japanese could be seen at Angel Island and Tule Lake (California), Camp McCoy (Wisconsin), Camp Forrest (Tennessee), Camp Livingstone (Louisiana), Camp Shelby (Mississippi), Fort Sill (Oklahoma), Fort Missoula (Montana), Lordsburg and Santa Fe (New Mexico), Crystal City and Seagoville (Texas), Jerome (Arkansas), and Topaz (Utah). At times, a solitary gravestone was the only evidence of that trail of the uprooted. Poet Keiho Soga asked:

> When the war is over
> And after we are gone
> Who will visit
> This lonely grave in the wild
> Where my friend lies buried? [39]

Who indeed will visit? Who indeed will remember? Who indeed will care? Perhaps the sojourn of Suikei Furuya typified the mainland experience of Hawaii's

38. Okihiro, *Cane Fires*, pp. 253–54; and Gary Y. Okihiro, *Margins and Mainstreams: Asians in American History and Culture* (Seattle: University of Washington Press, 1994), pp. 41–42.

39. Nakano and Nakano, *Poets behind Barbed Wire*, p. 64.

internees. Furuya wrote about conflicts in crowded barracks among "mentally strained" men, of makeshift huts that leaked and flooded when it rained, of bedding that was filthy and stinking. But he also remembered the joy of receiving letters from home, of baseball games and an evening lecture series, and of watching the glow of fireflies at Camp Forrest, which made him feel so relaxed "that I forgot the hard conditions that I was placed [in]." Moved to Camp Livingstone, Furuya met highly educated Japanese who organized "Internee College," and he wrote about meeting Germans, Italians, and Peruvian Japanese at Fort Missoula, where he played baseball, golfed, fished, and saw movies. Gifts of books, green tea, *shoyu*, *miso*, and medicines from the Japanese Red Cross made Christmas Day 1943 especially memorable, and he wrote: "We were so grateful for their kindness that we didn't know how to express [it] in words."

Furuya left Montana for Santa Fe on April 3, 1944. There he joined about 800 other internees from Hawaii. Reflecting upon his four years of life in America's concentration camps, Furuya observed: "We learned a lot. . . . We learned to appreciate our wives. . . . We found that those who were respected in our communities turned out to be completely opposite of what we expected them to be, whereas there were others whom we thought idle but we found beautiful personalities among them." Yearning for the freedom of the skies above and of the wide open spaces beyond the barbed-wire fence, Furuya searched the vicinity of the camp. "One day, to my surprise," he recalled, "I found a quiet grass field. . . . I began to go there in the evenings and looked at the endless view of Santa Fe Plateau."[40]

Meanwhile, following the forced removal of the islanders at Terminal Island to the south and Bainbridge Island to the north, the army began the systematic uprooting of the entire West Coast Japanese population, about 110,000 people. The plans were formulated during a time when hearings were being held by Representative John H. Tolan of California in late February and early March 1942 in Seattle, Portland, San Francisco, and Los Angeles. The public forums achieved their purpose of informing Americans of the need for the internment of enemy aliens and for the mass removal of the Japanese, and they also served to distance Germans and Italians from the Japanese.[41] The majority of the testimony favored the mass incarceration of America's Japanese but insisted that "racial guilt" must not be applied to

40. Okihiro, *Cane Fires*, pp. 260–62.
41. See Stephen Fox, *The Unknown Internment: An Oral History of the Relocation of Italian Americans during World War II* (Boston: Twayne Publishers, 1990), for an account of the internment of Italians, and John Christgau, *"Enemies": World War II Alien Internment* (Ames: Iowa State University Press, 1985), for an account of the internment of Germans.

Europeans. A San Francisco attorney, Chauncey Tramutolo, argued that surely the DiMaggio parents, with professional baseball star sons Joe, Dominic, and Vincent, should not be evicted simply because they failed to naturalize and become American citizens. But as for the Japanese, city of Madera officials explained, "it is impossible for the police . . . to tell which Japanese are dangerous and which are not. . . . [Thus] the only safe procedure would be to take up all the Japanese and intern them."

Witnesses before the Tolan Committee, however, were not uniformly in favor of racial guilt for the Japanese. Tacoma mayor Harry P. Cain insisted upon judging each person, "regardless of who he is," individually, and the Committee on National Security and Fair Play, a group of religious leaders and educators, declared that the *nisei* who were American citizens by birth should not be given "less consideration than German and Italian aliens." And A. L. Wirin, southern California counsel for the American Civil Liberties Union, argued "that persons must be judged, so long as we have a Bill of Rights, because of what they do as persons. . . . We feel that treating persons, because they are members of a race, constitutes illegal discrimination, which is forbidden by the fourteenth amendment whether we are at war or peace."[42]

The Tolan hearings were crucial for the building of a national consensus on the mass removal of America's Japanese. Not all Americans favored that government action; not all Americans believed in its necessity. A government survey in California at the end of January 1942, for example, found that 36 percent believed the Japanese to be "virtually all loyal" while 38 percent thought them to be "virtually all disloyal." Although many of those surveyed felt a "certain amount of suspicion" toward the Japanese as an entire group because they could not distinguish the loyal from the disloyal among them, the majority of the respondents believed that the existing controls were adequate, and only one-third called for more government action against the Japanese. By the end of February 1942, over half of those surveyed questioned Japanese American loyalty, and fully 77 percent disliked and distrusted the Japanese on racial or national lines. Still, 54 percent held that government measures against the Japanese were adequate, although that number declined to 40 percent by the end of the month. At the close of the Tolan Committee's work in March, a national survey found that 93 percent approved the internment of Japa-

42. Daniels,
Concentration Camps,
pp. 74–79.

nese aliens, and 59 percent favored the removal of all Japanese, aliens and citizens alike.[43] The public had gotten the message, and the way was now prepared.

"We, the permanent Japanese resident nationals in this county of Hood River, do express to you and through you to the federal, state and local officials, and to the American people at large, our heartfelt and sincere gratitude for the generous treatment accorded us by our courteous American friends," began a declaration signed by 148 *issei* and addressed to Oregon's governor during the period when the federal government contemplated their fate. "Most of the alien Japanese residents are devoted to this great Democratic America though we are not eligible for citizenship," the petitioners explained. "We love this country so much that we wish to live here permanently, obeying American laws, policies, and administration always and especially during the present situation; and to cooperate whole-heartedly, endeavoring to prove our destinies common with that of the American public." They concluded: "May we pledge our loyalty to the Stars and Stripes just as do our children who are patriotic American citizens, with our prayer for a more peaceful kingdom on earth, which is the divine bequest of the American people for future generations."[44]

Beginning in the north and sweeping southward, the army and its civilian agency the Wartime Civil Control Administration forcibly evicted all the Japanese living in California and parts of Washington, Oregon, and Arizona. The deed was completed by August 1942. Given weeks and sometimes days to prepare for their removal, most of the Japanese suffered heavy financial losses. "Hearing a lot of rumors from my customers every day," recalled Riyo Orite, "I felt uneasy. They tried to encourage me, but I felt helpless about the boarding house and procrastinated about closing this business. My husband had died the year before, and it was a difficult time. Then the evacuation came along. It was awful. Because of racial prejudice, people threw rocks at us, and I was scared and worried." Orite eventually closed down her boardinghouse and left it "almost free of charge. It couldn't be helped. I only got paid one hundred and fifty dollars for a sixty-room building. I had no choice in the matter."[45]

Shoichi Fukuda remembered: "We had just purchased a good stove, a piano, and a radio. We had to sell these things we owned very cheaply. Many white people came

43. Gary Y. Okihiro and Julie Sly, "The Press, Japanese Americans, and the Concentration Camps," *Phylon* 44, no. 1 (1983): 78.
44. Quoted in Linda Tamura, *The Hood River Issei: An Oral History of Japanese Settlers in Oregon's Hood River Valley* (Urbana: University of Illinois Press, 1993), pp. 151–52.
45. Sarasohn, *Issei,* pp. 168–69.

into homes and asked the occupants to leave their things for them. They knew that the Japanese people had to evacuate and sell whatever they owned at a loss. . . . For instance, the stove for which we paid two hundred dollars was sold for fifteen. It was the same with the radio, washing machine, and all other tools and appliances. We had to sell everything so cheaply that it was just like throwing things away." Others, like Riichi Satow, packed all their belongings in one room of their house, asked someone to watch it for them, and rented out the home. Tei Endow loaned her prized chinaware to her White friends instead of selling it.[46]

"We were herded onto the train just like cattle and swine," recounted Misuyo Nakamura. "I do not recall much conversation between the Japanese. But I do remember sitting next to Etsuko Abe from Parkdale, who offered to share a lunch she had made. My thinking was, 'My goodness, how well this person prepared!'" Tei Endow recalled: "Our departure was somewhat quiet and reserved. Everyone seemed willing to express good feelings rather than bitter ones. Naturally we did not like what was happening," she explained, "but we tried to suppress our feelings and leave quietly and with goodwill. . . . The train we boarded was so old-fashioned that we thought it might have come from a museum! Once inside, we all talked and talked, curious about where we were going. My five-year-old son thought it was great to ride on a train! But my husband and I commiserated with Mr. and Mrs. Tamura, crying together about our fate."[47]

"I cannot speak for others, but I myself felt resigned to do whatever we were told. I think the Japanese left in a very quiet mood, for we were powerless," explained Misuyo Nakamura. "We had to do what the government ordered." The night before their departure, Nakamura and the other mothers must have wandered through the empty rooms of their houses, straining to hear, above the deafening echo of their footsteps, the laughter of children, and yearning to feel, amid the lifeless chill, the warmth of friends and family for possibly the last time. They must have looked back, as the car drove them off to the train station, to catch a final glimpse of their homes. "In my own mind, I thought, 'Surely we will be unable to return,'" she admitted. "I was so worried about what the future held for my children! We had struggled for many years, but we could lose everything. I was so frightened I actually did not think we would come home alive. . . . We took just one day at a time."[48]

46. Ibid., pp. 169, 171–72; and Tamura, *Hood River Issei*, p. 166.
47. Tamura, *Hood River Issei*, pp. 167–68.
48. Ibid., p. 169.

"Now it was noon, and we did the last-minute chores," wrote Shuji Kimura of his last day at the family farm in Auburn, Washington. "Father fed the horse an extra gallon of barley. Then we loaded our truck with our and a neighbor's luggage, and started for the train. The 18-car train was drawn up in the siding along the packing house from which we used to ship our peas and lettuce, and the place was full of people. There was a tremendous line-up of trucks loaded with baggage. . . . Many friends had come to see us off." The commotion and excitement at the station temporarily blunted the sharpness of the occasion. "But soon when six P.M. came and the train began to move, and we saw old Mr. Ballard waving his hat at us, his coat collar turned up against the rain, Mother began to cry. I couldn't see through my tears either. . . . The train began to go faster and the berry rows, the rhubarb, the lettuce fields, the pea fields began to slip past our window like a panorama. My throat hurt, but I couldn't take my eyes from the family fields and pastures slipping so quickly away."[49]

Kathleen Shimada described the train ride to Pinedale Assembly Center. "All I can remember is its being so dirty and rattly, miserable and cold," she said. "Day wasn't bad, but at night we had to sleep in the chairs, just sitting with the blanket we had with us, frightened and depressed. The whole thing was just miserable. I was bitter then for being uprooted from my home and taken off. We didn't know where we were going. I think it would have been easier if I had had my dad but, you see, I was the oldest of five with only my mother. The future is pretty bleak when you are uprooted from your home, not knowing where to go, and the responsibility lies on your shoulders."[50]

"On April 24, 1942, Civilian Exclusion Order No. 19 was issued and posted everywhere in Berkeley. Our turn had come," reported artist Mine Okubo. The army's sweep, begun in Washington, had marched down through Oregon and into California. Two days later, Okubo reported to a civil control station set up at the First Congregational Church, where she was interviewed by a woman who "asked me many questions and filled in several printed forms as I answered. As a result of the interview, my family name was reduced to No. 13660. I was given several tags bearing the family number, and was then dismissed." The following week, she was given three days to pack. "My brother," she wrote, "was excused from the Univer-

49. Girdner and Loftis, *Great Betrayal*, pp. 139-40.

50. Ibid., p. 142.

sity with a promise that he would receive his B.A. degree in June. Our friends came to cheer us up and to wish us luck. It was like old home week but we were exhausted from work and worry. On the last morning the main part of the packing was finished but there was still plenty to be done. I asked different friends to take care of some of my cherished possessions. In the last hour I dashed to the bank to get some money, picked up my laundry, and paid my household bills." After tagging their bags, Okubo and her brother were ready. But before leaving, she recalled, "we took one last look at our happy home."

"The entire city block around the Civil Control Station was guarded by military police," she continued. "Baggage was piled on the sidewalk the full length of the block. Greyhound buses were lined alongside the curb." At the station, Okubo was absorbed by the hundreds of people already there, standing in line, receiving sandwiches and fruit from church people, and stepping into a bus when their numbers were called. She had become part of a faceless mass. "Many spectators stood around," she noted. "At that moment I recalled some of the stories told on shipboard by European refugees bound for America. We were silent on the trip except for a group of four University of California boys who were singing college songs. The bus crossed the Bay Bridge. Everyone stared at the beautiful view as if for the last time. The singing stopped."[51]

Although nearly all of them went, a few Japanese refused. Hideo Murata, according to editor and writer Carey McWilliams, was a veteran of World War I and had been presented with a "Certificate of Honorary Citizenship" by the Monterey County Board of Supervisors because of his service in the war. "Monterey County presents this testimony of heartfelt gratitude, of honor and respect for your loyal and splendid service to the country in the Great World War," the certificate read. "Our flag was assaulted, and you gallantly took up its defense." When notices were posted in the county instructing the Japanese to ready themselves for removal, Murata went to see his friend the sheriff to ask him if the notices were a mistake or a practical joke. Upon discovering the seriousness of the order, Murata "went to a local hotel, paid for his room, and committed suicide. The sheriff found the certificate of honorary citizenship clutched in his hand."[52]

In April 1942, even before the mass removal orders were posted, Mary Asaba

51. Mine Okubo, *Citizen 13660* (New York: Columbia University Press, 1946), pp. 17–26.
52. Carey McWilliams, *Prejudice: Japanese-Americans, Symbol of Racial Intolerance* (Boston: Little, Brown, 1944), p. 133.

186

Ventura, a *nisei* married to a Filipino and a resident of Seattle, challenged in court the military curfew orders that she claimed unreasonably infringed upon her rights as a loyal and devoted citizen. The federal district judge denied her petition, trivializing her contention as "some technical right of [a] petitioning wife to defeat the military needs in this vital area during this extraordinary time." A fellow Seattle *nisei*, Gordon Hirabayashi, deliberately refused to comply with the curfew orders and failed to report for "evacuation." He was held in jail for five months before his trial, where he was found guilty on both counts by the same judge who had heard Ventura's case earlier.

Hood River, Oregon, native Minoru Yasui, like Hirabayashi, purposefully violated the curfew order to challenge its legality. He was found guilty and sentenced to a year's imprisonment; Yasui spent more than nine months in solitary confinement. Fred Korematsu of Oakland, California, refused to report for "evacuation," was spotted on the street and arrested by San Leandro police, and was found guilty of violating the military exclusion order. The challenges by Hirabayashi, Yasui, and Korematsu were eventually heard by the U.S. Supreme Court, and the judgments against them became the legal pillars that upheld the entire program of mass removal and detention.[53]

Japanese blood was the criterion that determined removal by the military. In San Francisco, two children, part Japanese and one with blond hair and blue eyes, were taken from their White mother and sent with their estranged father, whom they hardly knew, to the assembly center. As the mother began crying hysterically, a witness recounted, an official lectured the crowd, "Now, don't you people go and get into this."[54]

But there were those who were just as violently left behind. "I remember Mrs. Kuima," said Mary Tsukamoto, "whose son was thirty-two years old and retarded. She took care of him. They had five other boys, but she took care of this boy at home. The welfare office said No, she couldn't take him, that the families had to institutionalize a child like that. It was a very tragic thing for me to have to tell her, and I remember going out to the field—she was hoeing strawberries—and I told her what they told us, that you can't take your son with you. And so she cried, and I cried with her." They took her son away a few days before "evacuation," and about

53. Daniels, *Concentration Camps*, pp. 131–43; and Peter Irons, *Justice at War: The Story of the Japanese American Internment Cases* (New York: Oxford University Press, 1983).
54. Girdner and Loftis, *Great Betrayal*, p. 139.

a month after the family had been moved to Fresno Assembly Center, the Kuimas received word that their son had died. "All these years she loved him and took care of him," reflected Tsukamoto; "he only knew Japanese and ate Japanese food. I was thinking of the family; they got over it quietly; they endured it." [55]

Although many of the exiles believed that they might never again see their beloved homes and communities, others grew even more determined to reclaim their birthright. "You had an uncertainty about where you were going and what was going to happen," said Fuji Takaichi, "but you knew you weren't going to be killed. . . . We went by train to Santa Anita about five o'clock in the afternoon. The train to Los Angeles goes down the coast by way of Monterey near the highway we had traveled so often. The sun was just going down. I remember looking out under the shade and saying to myself, 'This is mine, my country. I don't care, I'm coming back.' " [56] That promise to come back was finally kept because of the efforts of the Japanese themselves and because of the deeds of others.

Besides the White neighbors and friends who helped store things for the Japanese, looked after their houses and farms, and managed their financial accounts, other courageous Whites worked as best they could to ease the pain inflicted by the government. In San Jose, White women from the First Presbyterian Church and Young Women's Christian Association offered hot coffee to the adults, milk to the children, and fruit as the Japanese boarded the train, and other White women came to the station "to say goodbye to Japanese friends and wish them well." [57] And in Berkeley, even before the mass removal, a group composed of educators, students, and church members formed the Student Relocation Committee, which succeeded in placing West Coast Japanese American students in universities and colleges east of the restricted areas. In May 1942, the National Japanese American Student Relocation Council was formed, with college presidents and deans, leaders of many Protestant churches, Jews, Catholics, and Quakers, and the student YMCA and YWCA among its members. Sustained by funds mainly from church groups and private foundations, the council placed over 4,000 *nisei* students in 600 institutions and thereby played a major role in preserving the education and future of an entire generation. [58]

A grateful *nisei*, Yuzuro Sato, probably spoke for his generation: "One may say if

55. Tateishi, *And Justice for All*, pp. 8–9.
56. Girdner and Loftis, *Great Betrayal*, p. 142.
57. Lukes and Okihiro, *Japanese Legacy*, pp. 119–20.
58. National Japanese American Student Relocation Council, *From Camp to College: The Story of Japanese American Student Relocation* (Philadelphia: National Japanese American Student Relocation Council, n.d.).

we struggle through this interlude, we will find haven in the fact that we will emerge a stronger and wiser people," he declared while still confined in a concentration camp. "Strength, courage, and wisdom will not alone be enough for us to lead our fellow Japanese Americans through the dark days ahead, during which time many will become destitute and many without fortitude will degenerate into uselessness. What the outlook of the younger generation will be—Heaven only knows. Those of us who are able must seek the wisdom of education—education to lead, to enlighten, and to carve for ourselves, at this time, an impregnable niche in our America . . . all I ask is a chance to play a part in the destiny of our country."[59] That opportunity was made possible by antiracist Whites such as Margaret Cosgrave Sowers, who volunteered her summers in Berkeley working for the original Student Relocation Committee because, as she said simply, the mass detention of America's Japanese was "such an obvious wrong."

Most of the uprooted were temporarily housed in places called assembly centers, often county fairgrounds and horse-racing tracks, before they were moved to the ten concentration camps run by the War Relocation Authority (WRA), the successor to the Wartime Civil Control Administration. Japanese from the north bay were sent to the Tanforan racetrack in San Bruno just south of San Francisco. "The gates were opened by military guards and the bus drove into the Tanforan Race Track grounds," wrote Mine Okubo. "Baggage of all sizes and shapes was piled high along the driveway in back of the grandstand, and earlier arrivals were searching among the stacks for their possessions. We waited in the parked bus for fifteen minutes . . . the soldier got out and opened the door and we filed out past him."

The women and men were separated, and the latter were stripped and searched "from head to toe" for contraband, including razors, knives, and liquor. After medical examinations, Okubo and her brother were assigned to barrack 16, room 50. The ground was wet and muddy. Their guide took them to *stable* 16 and deposited them at *stall* 50. "We walked in and dropped our things inside the entrance," Okubo recalled. "The place was in semidarkness; light barely came through the dirty window on either side of the entrance. A swinging half-door divided the 20 by 9 ft. stall into two rooms. The roof sloped down from a height of twelve feet in the rear of the room to seven feet in the front room; below the rafters an open space ex-

59. Ibid.

189

tended the full length of the stable. The rear room had housed the horse and the front room the fodder. Both rooms showed signs of a hurried whitewashing. Spider webs, horse hair, and hay had been whitewashed with the walls. Huge spikes and nails stuck out all over the walls. A two-inch layer of dust covered the floor, but on removing it we discovered that linoleum the color of redwood had been placed over the rough manure-covered boards." Sitting in the semidarkness, Okubo wrote, "we heard someone crying in the next stall."[60]

"We went to the stable, Tanforan Assembly Center," recalled Osuke Takizawa. "It was terrible. The government moved the horses out and put us in. The stable stunk awfully. I felt miserable, but I couldn't do anything. It was like a prison, guards on duty all the time, and there was barbed wire all around us. We really worried about our future. I just gave up." "Though I was tired, I couldn't sleep because of the bad smell," added his wife, Sadae Takizawa. "It was hell. Everybody felt lonely and anxious about the future. In a word, we were confused. Deep down, we felt anger. It was a melancholy, complex feeling." Her husband explained: "I was all mixed-up. We couldn't do anything about the orders from the U.S. government. I just lived from day to day without any purpose. I felt empty. . . . I frittered away every day. I don't remember anything much. . . . I just felt vacant."

Sadae Takizawa put her thoughts into poetry during her confinement in the horse stall. "I composed verses expressing my feelings at Tanforan," she said quietly. Her poems reflected her everyday reality:

> People are crowded
> in a long line like a snake.
> The crowd is waiting for a meal
> in the dust and wind.

Her poems bared the inner rage:

> I recall Noah's flood
> in ancient times.
> Angry waves were surging
> in these days.

60. Okubo, *Citizen 13660*, pp. 27–36.

190

Her poems were mirrors into which she peered:

Because I am
a Japanese woman,
I should stand firmly
at all times.[61]

After sitting in the semidarkness of their stall, Mine Okubo and her brother began sweeping the "two-inch layer of dust" that covered their floor. At 4 P.M. they, along with 5,000 others, rushed to the grandstand for supper. "When we arrived, four lines, each a block long, waited outside the mess-hall doors," she noted hopelessly. "It was very windy and cold. An hour passed and we finally reached the door only to learn that the line did not lead anywhere." The thought of starting all over again at the end of another line was too much to bear, so they cut into a line when they spotted a friend. "People glared at us," she reported, "as we squeezed into line." When she reached the counter, Okubo held out her plate and received boiled potatoes, no Vienna sausages because they had just run out of them, and two slices of bread. Her ordeal had just begun. She was "pushed" into the dining area, where "a bedlam of hungry people" occupied every table and chair, and where the air was so stuffy that she lost her appetite. She put down her plate and left. Some time later, she returned to the mess hall to find that the place had cleared, and this time she got canned hash with her potato and two slices of bread. She sat down and had her first meal in the center.

After dinner, Okubo and her brother ran to meet the Bekins trucks that brought their luggage. "Packages and boxes came hurtling out; some of them split open as they hit the ground," she wrote. They finally located their suitcases; the cover of one "was torn loose from the hinges." A truck transported them and their luggage to their stable, and they dragged their stuff to their stall. With night approaching, Okubo and her brother headed for the "mattress department" about a half mile away. There they were given loosely sewn bags filled with straw, and they struggled back to their stall carrying their "awkward load" in the wind and dust. Before turning in and still hungry, the Okubos opened a can of peaches and some crackers

61. Sarasohn, *Issei*, pp. 183–85.

191

which they had packed in their luggage on the advice of friends who had told them to bring food with them to the center.

"We 'hit the hay' around ten that night," Okubo wrote, "but learned very quickly that sleep was not to be easily won. Because the partitions were low and there were many holes in the boards they were made of, the crackling of the straw and the noises from the other stalls were incessant. Loud snores, the grinding of teeth, the wail of babies, the murmur of conversations—these could be heard the full length of the stable. Moreover, it was very cold and we were shivering." The pair unpacked their clothes, spread them over the single blanket they had been issued, and crawled into bed. "Sleep finally overtook us around midnight," sighed Okubo. "Thus ended our first day in the Tanforan Assembly Center." [62]

In Pinedale Assembly Center near Fresno, where the Hood River Japanese were taken, internees worried over their futures, endured trying physical conditions, and worked to return some dignity to their lives in the center called "Hell's Acre." Perhaps eleven-year-old George Nakamura best expressed the exiles' initial reaction to Pinedale when he first entered the family's assigned barrack. Misuyo Nakamura recalled that her son "was overcome with frustration by the dismal conditions. He became so disgusted that he threw himself on the concrete floor, screaming and pounding his feet! I can still picture George going through this motion. Our feeling were very similar to George's—but we did not express them," she confessed.

Pinedale greeted them after an exhausting, one-thousand-mile train ride. "Since we were on a train which did not have priority," explained Tei Endow, "we were constantly sidetracked to allow other trains to pass. Finally, at ten o'clock at night, the train stopped at an open field. We had to wade through the tall grass to reach Pinedale, and I cannot forget how the burrs snagged our stockings." Itsu Akiyama described her first impression of the place: "I remember seeing a large cactus when our train stopped at a field near Pinedale, so I guessed that we had arrived at a hot place. We were completely fenced in, and there were watchtowers with soldiers bearing rifles. We felt like prisoners!" "I saw a soldier with a rifle who was stationed on one of those high towers outside the fence," added Misuyo Nakamura. "I was very frightened! I was sure he had designs on shooting us!"

Akiyama's observation proved correct. Pinedale was unbearably hot. Tempera-

62. Okubo, *Citizen 13660*, pp. 37–47.

192

tures soared to 120 degrees in the shade. "It was a terribly hot place to live," recalled Hatsumi Nishimoto. "It was so hot that when we put our hands on the bedstead, the paint would come off! To relieve the pressure of the heat, some people soaked sheets in water and hung them overhead." Others threw water on the concrete floor and lay on the pools as the water evaporated. Besides the heat, the internees had to contend with rooms that afforded little privacy; straw-filled mattresses that were so uncomfortable, said Tei Endow, that she could not sleep; toilets without partitions; and food that was strange, unappetizing, and often left one still hungry after eating. "Frequently our meal was a plateful of white beans, four or five fresh spinach leaves, a piece of bread, and sometimes a couple of weinies," remembered Miyoshi Noyori. "That was all we were served, so we had to eat it."[63]

Despite the grimness of the centers, laughter could still be heard. Humor sometimes served as social commentary. "Yesterday," a young internee wrote, "there was so much dust that ten feet up in the air I saw a mole digging his burrow." While living in horse stables, the residents held a fly-catching contest in which the winner triumphantly displayed a gallon jug filled with 2,462 dead flies. "How I wish we had traps or cats for the rats and mice who play tag all over us in the dark!" exclaimed a resident of the Tanforan stables. Another stable dweller at Tanforan reasoned: "We had to make friends with the wild creatures in the camp, especially the spiders, mice, and rats, because we were outnumbered." People at Santa Anita vied for the "honor" of living in barrack 28, units 24 and 25, the stall once occupied by the famed horse Seabiscuit. At Manzanar, residents proudly displayed signs with the names of their barracks: Dusty Inn, Manzanar Mansion, Waldorf Astoria, and La Casa de Paz; and at Tanforan artist Mine Okubo put up a sign, "Quarantined—Do Not Enter," and when asked what she had, Okubo replied, "Hoof and mouth disease. Go away!"[64]

"Humor," Okubo observed, "is the only thing that mellows life, shows life as the circus it is. After being uprooted, everything seemed ridiculous, insane, and stupid. There we were in an unfinished camp, with snow and cold. The evacuees helped sheetrock the walls for warmth and built the barbed wire fence to fence themselves in. We had to sing 'God Bless America' many times with a flag. Guards all around with shot guns, you're not going to walk out. I mean . . . what could you do? So many crazy things happened in the camp. So the joke and humor I saw in the camp

63. Tamura, *Hood River Issei*, pp. 173-76.
64. Girdner and Loftis, *Great Betrayal*, pp. 148, 152, 153; Okubo, *Citizen 13660*, p. 68; Tamura, *Hood River Issei*, p. 177; and Uchida, *Desert Exile*, p. 96.

193

was not in a joyful sense, but ridiculous and insane. It was dealing with people and situations. . . . I tried to make the best of it, just adapt and adjust."[65]

Beauty and human dignity, like humor, could still be found in the camps. Women pinned up curtains and propped up boards for privacy in the open community toilets, and even though they realized that Tanforan was a temporary camp, volunteers planned a pond and park. Workers dug up trees and shrubs and transplanted them around the swampy ground that became a pond. They created islands and built a bridge and promenade. When it opened on August 2, 1942, "North Lake" "was a great joy to the residents and presented new material for the artists," Okubo recalled. "In the morning sunlight and at sunset it added great beauty to the bleak barracks."[66]

Still, after some time at Pinedale, nine- or ten-year-old Louie Tomita looked up and said, " 'Pa, go home, go home. I like to go home.' I can't say nothing—maybe someday go home," was his dad's hopeful response.[67]

But years of exile and confinement still awaited most of America's Japanese, and "home" had to be made and remade wherever they were directed and in whatever place they were able to secure for themselves. The poet Yukari described the agonizing process of coming to terms with the new reality.

> Four months have passed,
> And at last I learn
> To call this horse stall
> My family's home.[68]

65. Deborah Gesensway and Mindy Roseman, *Beyond Words: Images from America's Concentration Camps* (Ithaca: Cornell University Press, 1987), p. 71.
66. Okubo, *Citizen 13660*, pp. 74, 98–99.
67. Tamura, *Hood River Issei*, p. 176.
68. Uchida, *Desert Exile*, p. 83.

From assembly centers like Pinedale and Tanforan, Puyallup (Washington), Portland (Oregon), Marysville, Sacramento, Stockton, Turlock, Merced, Salinas, Fresno, Tulare, Santa Anita, and Pomona (California), and Camp Mayer (Arizona), the uprooted were transferred (or "transplanted" according to the April 6, 1942, issue of *Newsweek*, in reference to the general process of removal) to the ten WRA-run concentration camps: Tule Lake and Manzanar (California), Minidoka (Idaho), Topaz (Utah), Poston and Gila River (Arizona), Heart Mountain (Wyoming), Amache (Granada, Colorado), and Rohwer and Jerome (Arkansas).

"On the train to Manzanar, I was really irritated because of the conditions—

that train was old," recalled Tom Watanabe. "We stopped in Bishop, and then they transferred us into a bus and then they took us into camp. When we got into camp it was a feeling of like, you're lost. You don't know what the hell to do. You don't know who to communicate with. I mean it's like some guy just opened the door on a bus and put you out on a desert highway and said, 'Here it is, this is where you're going to live.' I mean you just don't know." Watanabe, his pregnant wife, his two sisters, and three other families, "people I never met in my life," shared a twenty-foot-square room. The four families partitioned off the room by hanging blankets, and they were given folding cots and straw-stuffed mattresses for their beds. "And that's when I started to rebel," declared Watanabe. "You know, you get so frustrated. I mean, you want to punch somebody, but there's nothing to do."[69]

Eddie Sakamoto heard that Manzanar was like "a different country," with mosquitoes as big as flies. Sakamoto's first impression was of confinement and loss of control over one's own life. "At the beginning there," he said, "I felt like a prisoner because they had four watchtowers, and the soldiers with their guns watching from on top of the tower. And anybody try to go out, not escaping, but try to go out, they shoot you, without giving any warning. In camp, the future is uncertain. You can't predict what's going to happen. I'm not against American government," he declared. "The government, we're trusting that they won't do any harmful decision; we trusting that American government will treat us maybe fair, you know."[70]

"When we got to Manzanar," recalled Yuri Tateishi, "it was getting dark and we were given numbers first. We went to the mess hall, and I remember the first meal we were given in those tin plates and tin cups. It was canned weiners and canned spinach. It was all the food we had, and then after finishing that we were taken to our barracks. It was dark and trenches were here and there. You'd fall in and get up and finally got to the barracks. The floors were boarded, but they were about a quarter to a half inch apart, and the next morning you could see the ground below. What hurt most I think was seeing those hay mattresses. We were used to a regular home atmosphere, and seeing those hay mattresses—so makeshift, with hay sticking out—a barren room with nothing but those hay mattresses. It was depressing, such a primitive feeling."[71]

The pitiful camp, spread out over 560 acres on which were constructed nine

69. Tateishi, *And Justice for All*, pp. 94–95.
70. Ibid., p. 17.
71. Ibid., pp. 24–25.

wards of four blocks each, with sixteen flimsily built barracks per block, mocked the timeless beauty of the mountains that surrounded it. "The next morning, the first morning in Manzanar, when I woke up and saw what Manzanar looked like, I just cried," remembered Haruko Niwa. "And then I saw the mountain, the high Sierra Mountain, just like my native country's mountain, and I just cried, that's all. I couldn't think about anything." Artist Kango Takamura described his first view of the camp. "We arrived at Manzanar in the early morning, before sunrise. Beautiful. All pink. The mountains around there were all pink. So beautiful. Yes, I thought this is such a nice place."[72]

Removed to the east of the mountains that were signifiers of both displacement and recentering, an anonymous poet celebrated the "magic" of the "western hills":

> Beyond those steel-blue western hills . . .
> California
> We huddle round the mesquite fire,
> We old Isseis at sunrise,
> In black coats,
> Gazing . . .
> Home.
> Dreaming at sunrise, our eyes are big.
> Why do our eyes become full?
>   Do memories make eyes full?
>   Does deep longing do this to eyes?
> Only the western hill we see — no others,
> Only the western hills have a glory,
>   A glory wet and brimming.
> Though their cold, steel blue shoulders blur as we gaze,
> Only the western hills have magic.
> Home.[73]

First impressions could mislead. Kango Takamura quickly learned that the camp, set beneath pink mountains, turned ugly in the changing light. He found just deso-

72. Ibid., p. 29; and Gesensway and Roseman, *Beyond Words*, p. 123.
73. Gesensway and Roseman, *Beyond Words*, pp. 24, 26.

lation in the barracks to which he was assigned. "Nobody was there," he noted. "Just snakes, such a wild place! Only the lumber was laid down, that's all. So we had to tar-paper and put waterlines in." And the physical conditions compounded his misery. "Oh, it's really so hot, you see, and the wind blows," he explained. "There's no shade at all. It's miserable, really. But one year after, it's quite a change," he added. "A year after they built the camp and put water there, the green grows up. And mentally everyone is better. That's one year after." [74]

Tom Watanabe described the dust storms that frequented Manzanar. "You had the dust storm come through. You get a half an inch of dust. You either get in bed and cover yourself with a sheet or just stand out there and suffer. You couldn't even see three feet in front of you, and then by the time the dust storm was settled, you had at least a half inch of dust right on your sheet when you got under it. Used to come from underneath the floor," he explained. "The floor used to have at least half an inch openings. The walls were nothing but one by sixes and tar paper." [75]

A child, Itsuko Taniguchi, described in a poem her journey to "the land with lots of sand":

> My Mom, Pop, & me
> Us living three
> Dreaded the day
> When we rode away,
> Away to the land
> With lots of sand
> My mom, pop, & me.
>
> The day of evacuation
> We left our little station
> Leaving our friends
> And my tree that bends
> Away to the land
> With lots of sand
> My mom, pop, & me. [76]

74. Ibid., pp. 123–24.
75. Tateishi, *And Justice for All*, p. 95.
76. Gesensway and Roseman, *Beyond Words*, pp. 91, 94.

The Japanese, "transplants" in this "land with lots of sand," responded in various ways. Some withered and died. Others struggled to bring greenness to the "wild place." Harry Ueno recalled how watching people stand in line outside the mess hall amid a dust storm one day gave him the idea of digging a pond to alleviate the boredom and discomfort of having to wait for their meals. He and others commenced work on digging "a great big hole" about eighty feet in length. A nurseryman, Akira Nishi, drew up plans for the pond and garden, and with a borrowed army truck, men dragged rocks several tons in weight and set them around the edge of the pond that looped in a figure eight. Workers added plants, tree stumps, and other objects to complete the project. "Ours was a beautiful pond," declared Ueno. Soon, others in neighboring Manzanar blocks dug ponds, seventeen or eighteen altogether, and held campwide contests for the best garden pool.[77]

Fourteen of the sixteen barracks composing a block were residential buildings. The others served as the mess hall, meeting and recreational hall, and communal kitchen and bathhouse. The residential barracks were divided into "apartments" of various sizes, but generally an apartment was twenty by twenty-five feet in dimension, and on average, eight people were assigned to it. Sometimes as many as eleven people occupied an apartment, depending on the size of the family. Furnishings included iron cots, straw-filled mattresses, and three army blankets per person. And Manzanar, the best outfitted of all the WRA camps, was the government's showcase of American "fair play" in its benign and gentle treatment of its Japanese.

Poston's three camps, built on an Indian reservation in the Arizona desert, were nicknamed by the internees Duston, Roaston, and Toaston. "People kept falling down. We thought it was Devil's Island!" exclaimed an internee of those being admitted into the camp in July. People commonly suffered from nosebleeds and heat stroke, and newcomers were greeted with ice water, salt tablets, and wet towels. As they were being "processed" by interviewers, the internees were described by an observer: "Men and women, still sweating, holding on to children and bundles try to think. A whirlwind comes and throws clouds of dust into the mess hall, into the water and into the faces of the people while papers fly in all directions. . . . The new arrivals are constantly urged to be quick." To gain entry into the camp, the Japanese swore "loyalty to the United States" and agreed to work "to contribute to the needs

77. Sue Kunitomi Embrey, Arthur A. Hansen, and Betty Kulberg Mitson, *Manzanar Martyr: An Interview with Harry Y. Ueno* (Fullerton: California State University Oral History Program, 1986), pp. 28–30.

of the nation and in order to earn a livelihood for myself and my dependents." They were then loaded, together with their baggage, onto trucks and taken to their quarters. The camp's associate director peered in an "apartment" into which a family had just moved. "An elderly mother who had been in a hospital some years sat propped on her baggage gasping and being fanned by two daughters, while her son went around trying to get a bed set up for her. The old lady later died," he reported.[78]

"We spray water in the rooms and wet our cots and we carry wet towels over the head whenever we go out," an internee said. "The people [have] lost their smile in their faces . . . they are panting and panting. . . . The other day one of the guards died of heat prostration. . . . Truthfully, I must say this scorching Hell is a place beyond description and beyond tears." A schoolteacher wrote in her diary: "Haven't had enough energy to write or do anything but try to keep cool and keep going. . . . Arrived Sunday afternoon . . . at one P.M. It was exactly 24 hours on that terrible train." Children suffered in the heat, she noted. A child was taken to the hospital in a delirium: "She fought furiously," the teacher wrote, and remained unconscious for over a day.[79]

Dust was another feature common to many of the concentration camps. Perhaps the "loose flour-like sand" of Topaz, which was everywhere and got into the eyes, mouths, noses, and lungs of everyone, was the most notorious. Yoshiko Uchida described her first dust storm in Topaz. "I happened to be in another block walking home with a friend when the wind suddenly gathered ominous strength," she recalled. "It swept around us in great thrusting gusts, flinging swirling masses of sand in the air and engulfing us in a thick cloud that eclipsed barracks only ten feet away." Her friend grabbed her hand and pulled her into a laundry room, "but even inside, the air was thick with dust. The flimsy structure shuddered violently with each blast of wind, and we could hear garbage cans and wooden crates being swept from the ground and slammed against the building. We waited more than an hour, silent and rigid with fear, but the storm didn't let up. I was afraid the laundry barrack might simply break apart and the howling wind would fling us out into the desert, but I was too terrified even to voice my thoughts." When the wind died down a bit, Uchida dashed outside. "As I ran," she wrote, "I couldn't breathe and the dust was choking me. But fear gave me strength to fight the storm." When she reached her "apart-

78. Alexander H. Leighton, *The Governing of Men* (Princeton: Princeton University Press, 1945), pp. 64–66.
79. Girdner and Loftis, *Great Betrayal*, p. 212.

ment," her hair, eyebrows, and eyelashes were white with dust, Uchida discovered, and her mouth was "filled with its chalky taste."[80]

Cold was another hardship to be overcome. Many of the camps were located in high deserts where the nights were crisp and the winters even colder. As early as September, new arrivals Eiichi Sakauye and his family saw the mercury drop to below zero at Heart Mountain concentration camp. They had no blankets that first night and had to huddle together to keep warm.[81] "The first snow fell in Topaz on October 13," wrote Mine Okubo. "The residents went wild with excitement; for most of them this was the first experience of snow." The potbellied stove, she noted, became the center of family gatherings, and despite the initial stir over the snow, it soon melted and "as the alkaline soil did not absorb water, the ground became a sticky mass of mud." Yoshiko Uchida remembered a succession of dust storms, rain squalls, and a severe snowstorm, all during the month of November at Topaz. "Snow blew in from the holes still remaining in our roof and it was impossible to endure the ten degree Fahrenheit temperatures even though we were bundled up in coats, scarves, and boots," she wrote. "My fingers and toes ached from the cold."[82]

With the onset of winter, the WRA, wrote Okubo, distributed military jackets to all of the camp's employed internees. "It was welcome if peculiar apparel — warm pea jackets and army uniforms, sizes 38 and 44, apparently left over from the First World War," she speculated. Nonetheless, the sight of men and women bundled in oversized U.S. military coats in central Utah must have been odd, and the need for proper-fitting clothing prompted a rush on catalog sales. The result, reported Okubo, was that "everyone was dressed alike, because of the catalog orders and the G.I. clothes."[83] Although sometimes humorous under conditions of choice, wearing the same clothing within America's concentration camps added to the drabness of the place and accentuated the feelings of confinement and loss of identity among the internees.

"People acted just like dumb sheep," observed Wataru Ishisaka, "because life was so disrupted and confused. They lost their human dignity and respect." As a camp policeman, Ishisaka witnessed a number of "shameful things," "like fooling around with other's wives."[84] Mary Tsukamoto remembered how during confinement people "got on each other's nerves," which led to conflicts. At the assembly

80. Uchida, *Desert Exile*, pp. 109, 112–13.
81. Girdner and Loftis, *Great Betrayal*, p. 227.
82. Okubo, *Citizen 13660*, pp. 145–48; and Uchida, *Desert Exile*, p. 124.
83. Okubo, *Citizen 13660*, pp. 151–53.
84. Sarasohn, *Issei*, p. 202.

center in Fresno, she said, "we heard language from over the partitions, language I didn't want my daughter to grow up hearing. There was talking back to parents, young people shouting, fathers shouting and angry. All of that made me hate people, and I was ashamed of being a part of a group of people who would be so hateful to each other."[85]

People's behavior changed in the camps, noted Masaji Kusachi. "Our biggest surprise at Tule Lake came when we late arrivals found our buildings stripped. Even the pressboard partitions in the room and the six-by-six-foot coal box were gone. . . . We believe that those who had arrived earlier had taken the wood to improve their own living quarters. So we were forced to scrounge around for other building materials. . . . It was such a strange period in our lives to be confined in those centers that our attitudes made a complete turnaround. At home we would never, never have given a thought to taking property from another person!" he declared. Kusachi realized that the uncertainties of the camps led people to hoard, steal, and seek the individual over the collective good simply for survival. "There was kind of a mutual feeling that we were trying to improve our own living conditions," he said.[86]

Iwato Itow, recalling the brutal conditions at Poston, exclaimed: "With all that kind of dirty treatment, we have to take all that, and they don't think nothing of it. Boy, talk about cruel! I mean, that's like taking a two- or three-year-old kid out in the desert and then tromping on and kicking him. That's pretty dirty, you know." Within the concentration camps, wrote Franklyn Sugiyama, "the people are like fish dynamited—they are helplessly stunned, floating belly up on the stream of life." Frank Watanabe worried about the breakdown in the parent-child relationship. "Discipline," he wrote, "is neglected because the parents in many cases have lost faith in themselves as well as in this country. Initiative, individual assurance and the will to succeed have been lost in the desert sands just as water evaporates in its intense heat."[87]

Hanna Kozasa isolated some of the causes for the breakdown of the Japanese American family within the camps. "The barbed wire fences, the armed sentries, the observation towers," she wrote, "increased our sense of frustration to the point that many have not been able to regain a proper perspective. The most alarming aspect of life in the centers is the demoralization it is working in the people. It is

85. Tateishi, *And Justice for All*, pp. 14-15.
86. Tamura, *Hood River Issei*, p. 182.
87. Tateishi, *And Justice for All*, p. 143; and McWilliams, *Prejudice*, p. 220.

sapping their initiative in a frightening manner," she reported. "The forced labor, with its low pay, indecent housing, inadequate food, the insecurity of their position in a post-war America, have contributed to a deterioration of family life that is beginning to show in a sharply increased juvenile delinquency—this among a people that had the lowest crime rate of any group in the United States."[88]

Confinement and rejection and the emotions they engendered were epitomized by the fence that circled the camp in "That Damned Fence," composed by an anonymous poet.

They've sunk in posts deep into the ground,
They've strung wires all the way around.
With machine gun nests just over there,
And sentries and soldiers everywhere!

We're trapped like rats in a wired cage
To fret and fume with impotent rage;
Yonder whispers the lure of the night
But that DAMNED FENCE assails our sight.

We seek the softness of the midnight air,
But that DAMNED FENCE in the floodlight glare
Awakens unrest in our nocturnal quest,
And mockingly laughs with vicious jest.

With nowhere to go and nothing to do,
We feel terrible, lonesome, and blue;
That DAMNED FENCE is driving us crazy,
Destroying our youth and making us lazy.

Imprisoned in here for a long, long time,
We know we're punished though we've committed no crime
Our thoughts are gloomy and enthusiasm damp,
To be locked up in a concentration camp.

88. McWilliams, *Prejudice*, pp. 220–21.

Loyalty we know and patriotism we feel,
To sacrifice our utmost was our ideal.
To fight for our country, and die, mayhap;
Yet we're here because we happen to be a Jap.

We all love life, and our country best,
Our misfortune's to be here in the west;
To keep us penned behind that DAMNED FENCE
Is someone's notion of National Defense!!![89]

Besides its meaning as symbol, the fence also was a deadly border that demarcated the free from the unfree. As he approached the fence at Topaz, James Wakasa was shot and killed by a military police sentry at about 7:30 P.M. on Sunday, April 11, 1943. Wakasa, according to a guard, disregarded four warnings and continued to walk as if to escape when he was shot with a single bullet that pierced his chest. Wakasa was a sixty-three-year-old *issei* bachelor who had graduated from Tokyo's Keio College in 1900. Karl Akiya, a friend of Wakasa, recalled having dinner with him the evening of the fatal shooting. They liked to converse in Japanese, Akiya said, and reminisce about Japan. After the meal, Wakasa decided to go for a stroll, and it was highly unlikely that he tried to escape, noted Akiya, because there was no place to go.[90]

In another sense, life, for many *issei*, ended in the concentration camp. "The life of most of us Issei is now well spent," observed Akana Imamura. "We stand in the evening of life where there is no hope—the hope attributed to the Phoenix which brings a new vibrant life out of the ashes of the old." Kiyoshi Okamoto told about "an old man" at Heart Mountain who came to America about forty years before World War II, began as a railroad worker, pioneered in Alaska's fish canneries, labored in the fields of California's Imperial Valley, and became a shopkeeper in Los Angeles' Little Tokyo. Throughout, he and his wife maintained their self-respect and contributed to their children's education. "Today, he is sick in bed," wrote Okamoto. "He admits that he may not live until spring. He visualizes the little cemetery

89. Gesensway and Roseman, *Beyond Words*, pp. 64–65.
90. Sandra C. Taylor, *Jewel of the Desert: Japanese American Internment at Topaz* (Berkeley and Los Angeles: University of California Press, 1993), pp. 136–46.

on the bleak hillside back of our camp, where a small dozen have already preceded him. Despite his stoicism, there is something that bothers him. He was pauperized at the time of evacuation; his children are still minors; his wife cannot earn a living. What is to become of them after this winter?"[91]

It is a difficult thing to come to the end of one's productive life and see the fruits of one's labor disappear in the desert dust. But it is even more difficult to believe that the future holds no promise for the next generation, for the children, no promise of spring. A mother, Ellen Kiskiyama, penned her love in a letter, "To My Son, Arthur." "Listen my son," she wrote, "now that you are older, Mother wants you to understand why your only friends are the sanseis [third-generation Japanese] and why your only home is the barrack—why you eat in the mess halls and why you don't ride the street cars, busses and automobiles." Pearl Harbor, Kiskiyama began, changed "our plans." The family sold their new car, gas range, refrigerator, rugs, sofa, dad's collection of rare tropical fish, and mom's more than forty dolls from China, Korea, Manchuria, and Hawaii. "Little by little," she recalled, "our home was broken up and all the fancy dreams we planned for you had to be altered."

Arthur's birth in the Pomona Assembly Center brought boundless joy to mom and dad, Kiskiyama continued, but was greeted with the headline "First Jap Baby Swells Center Population" in the local newspapers. "Being a camp baby, we had no baby picture of you until a news photographer snapped one on your 100th day—and that is the only picture we have of you," Kiskiyama sadly told her son. She informed him of a family whom he never knew, of an uncle who served in the U.S. Army and of cousins scattered about in Manzanar, Poston, Gila River, and Minidoka. "Your first Christmas was observed in camp," Kiskiyama wrote, "and Mother took you to see the nice Santa Claus and the colored lights and the prettily decorated tree. You with your tiny friends had a merry time and received your gift from Santa. And so each day rolled into weeks and weeks into months and months into years—You look tired and sleepy now, my son. Go to sleep and dream of the glorious future we will plan together," she wished him. "Good night, my son, Arthur."[92]

Only those who defied the darkness could dare to dream. *Nisei* writer Toyo Suyemoto asked:

91. McWilliams, *Prejudice*, p. 204.
92. Ibid., pp. 227–28.

Can this hard earth break wide
  The stiff stillness of snow
And yield me promise that
  This is not always so?

Surely the warmth of sun
  Can pierce the earth ice-bound
Until grass comes to life
  Outwitting barren ground![93]

For many, the act of creating restored a semblance of self-control and self-defini-tion. Inscribing one's tracings upon the "hard earth" helped to dispel the darkness. Hanayo Inouye remembered the awful heat and terrible dust storms at Poston, but "we were Japanese after all," she offered, "so no one spent lazy days. Some people planted various kinds of trees in the compound, and between the trees we grew vegetables and other things. When we first came to the camp, we all wondered what was going to happen to us. But when we were leaving, people were even saying that living in the camp was better than where they had come from. The trees had grown very big by then, and we could find nice shade under them and everything."[94]

Gardens transformed the desert into places of beauty. Even the alkaline soil could not resist this labor of love. Using sticks, stones, and native trees, shrubs, cacti, and flowers, along with the seeds sent to them by the American Friends Ser-vice Committee, the Japanese landscaped their blocks, erected hedges and facades around their barracks, and planted cactus and flower gardens that masked the bleak surroundings and pitiful tar-paper barracks. "In some camps," wrote an observer, "hardly a stick or stone was available; nevertheless, the note of beauty had to be achieved, and *was* achieved, through the use of strings and vines. Morning-glories, pumpkin vines and gourds transformed hundreds of barren entrances into bowers of enchantment." Y. Kogita of Minidoka took about two months to haul rocks, one weighing about 1,000 pounds, from as far as two miles away for his rock garden. "It was all very rough work," a reporter noted, "but most people think the result was worth it."[95]

93. Gesensway and Roseman, *Beyond Words*, pp. 46–47. Reprinted from Toyo Suyemoto, "In Topaz," *Trek Literary Magazine*, Feb. 1943, Manuscripts Division, Marriott Library, University of Utah.
94. Sarasohn, *Issei*, p. 196.
95. Allen H. Eaton, *Beauty behind Barbed Wire: The Arts of the Japanese in Our War Relocation Camps* (New York: Harper & Brothers, 1952), pp. 50–53, 92–95.

Family gardens were also a means by which to ensure an adequate and nutritious food supply. Although the food in Poston was generally "pretty good," reported Hanayo Inouye, her son Ben "lost so much weight and turned so pale that I thought he might be dying. It worried me a lot," she remembered. Her husband grew lots of spinach for their son. "Until that time," said Inouye, "the shortage of fresh produce was a big problem. Pretty soon Ben started regaining his normal color."[96] Mine Okubo described gardening at Topaz. "Despite reports that the alkaline soil was not good for agricultural purposes," she wrote, "in the spring practically everyone set up a victory garden. Some of the gardens were organized, but most of them were set up anywhere and any way. Makeshift screens were fashioned out of precious cardboard boxes, cartons, and scraps of lumber to protect the plants from the whipping dust storms."[97]

Inside the barracks, internees transformed barren, cheerless cells into tidy homes. They put up walls where there were once only exposed two-by-four support frames, painted and papered them, carved out niches and added shelves, and built *shoji* screens to cover the windows and keep out the sun's glare. Using scrap lumber, including shipping crates, many constructed tables, chairs, dressers, and other furniture for their "apartments." "Papa spent most of his time in carpentry," recalled Asayo Noji. "He built a lot of furniture for our apartment, including a double-decker bed to save space, a heavy dresser with drawers, a lamp, and a folding screen decorated with carvings and a Japanese scene. . . . Papa gave away little tables and a lot of wooden vases—all shapes and sizes. He felt so much joy giving away his hand-crafted goods!"[98]

Ko Takakoshi said that when she got to Minidoka "there was nothing to do in camp, so I started to teach children how to make flowers from orange wrappings. We gathered pieces of wire and got the orange wrappings from the mess halls. . . . I wasn't an expert," she modestly added, "but friends still tell me what a fine job I did. We also made paper flowers to send to Alaska. We sent poinsettias for Christmas, lilies for Easter, and carnations for other occasions. People were very appreciative of this, and I was happy that I was able to do it."[99] Classes and arts and crafts groups frequently started simply because of the skills and interests of people like Takakoshi.

The dust storms and ever-present sand at Amache inspired Mrs. Ninomiya to

96. Sarasohn, *Issei*, p. 196.
97. Okubo, *Citizen 13660*, p. 192.
98. Eaton, *Beauty behind Barbed Wire*, pp. 36–37, 54–55; and Tamura, *Hood River Issei*, p. 187.
99. Sarasohn, *Issei*, p. 199.

create a miniature landscape (*bon-kei*), an art form she had learned in Japan in which sand is a vital ingredient. With a box made for her by her neighbor, Ninomiya completed the camp's first *bon-kei*, which caused quite a stir among the women in her block, who asked her to teach them. Soon, word spread throughout the camp, and Ninomiya found herself with ninety-two students. Together, Ninomiya and her pupils held a camp exhibition of *bon-kei*. "Some of the tray gardens were of mountain, desert, and seacoast subjects," wrote a reporter, "but most of them were imaginary Japanese scenes; and in no cases were there any duplicates." For most of the women who eagerly created *bon-kei*, observed the writer, "there was the fascination of making something beautiful out of the commonest materials, and here sand was that commonest thing."[100]

Many of the arts flourished in the camps. "There were all kinds of classes at camp: flower arranging, haiku, tea ceremony, sewing," declared Itsu Akiyama. "Nearly every day Hamada-san, Sato-san, and I walked to the wooded area just outside camp to find materials for ikebana," Asayo Noji recalled. "We were allowed in the surrounding area without special permits, and we always returned with armloads of sagebrush and willow to share with others. Creating tranquil ikebana gave me much pleasure! Sometimes I worked until midnight to find a suitable branch or flower to give the right effect." Hatsumi Nishimoto remembered her sewing and embroidery classes taught by an eighty-five-year-old man "who did not even have to wear glasses!" she exclaimed.[101]

Indeed, Japanese Americans did not discover the arts in the concentration camps. Camp art was made possible because artists painted, wrote poetry, planted gardens, wove and embroidered, arranged flowers, and brushed calligraphy long before World War II. Those artists continued their work in the camps and inspired a resurgence of culture and a restoration of cultural identity among a bruised and battered people. Violet Matsuda de Cristoforo explained why she wrote haiku at Tule Lake. "Under the harsh conditions of camp life, stripped of dignity, self-respect and purpose, and with no access to radios or outside newspapers," she wrote, "rumor was rife and our lives were subject to uncertainty and doubt. It was only 'Gaman'—our ability to endure hardship and humiliation without complaint—that enabled us to survive. But, under those oppressive conditions, I became more and more intro-

100. Eaton, *Beauty behind Barbed Wire*, pp. 16–17.
101. Tamura, *Hood River Issei*, pp. 185–86.

spective and found solace in my Haiku as the humble expression of the dejection experienced by a lonely young mother with small children."[102]

The haiku group at Tule Lake, according to de Cristoforo, consisted of former members of the Valley Ginsha Haiku Kai started by Neiji Ozawa in the early 1930s. The Haiku Kai's members included "grape growers, onion farmers, teachers, housewives, bankers, pharmacists, and other community members" in the Fresno, California, area, who met monthly at members' homes to read their poems, critique them, and select the best haiku read that evening. At the war's outbreak, many poets destroyed their haiku and collections of Japanese literature, knowing that the bearers of Japanese culture were among the targets of the FBI's internment program. During the mass detention, the Haiku Kai's members were scattered in camps like Gila River and Jerome, but a number were sent to Tule Lake, where they formed the core of a reconstituted poetry group. When some of the key members were transferred from Tule Lake in December 1944, the "once energetic free-style haiku group, which had been known for its international flavor and capable women poets," was finally destroyed.[103]

Some of the visual artists who taught painting in the camp schools and adult classes had distinguished careers before the war. Chiura Obata arrived in San Francisco in 1906 and became an art professor at the University of California, Berkeley, in 1931. He founded art schools at Tanforan and Topaz and organized his students, including his former Berkeley students, into an influential group of art teachers who taught and painted in the camps to create a record for future generations. Gene Sogioka worked as background artist for Walt Disney Studios on films such as *Fantasia*, *Dumbo*, and *Bambi*. "The picture I worked on real hard is *Dumbo*," he recalled. "We all have imagination. You have to have imagination. You have to create something. That's how I feel even today," he declared. "If you don't have the imagination, creativity, you're dead." Sogioka described his watercolors depicting everyday life in Poston: "I sketched everything about the camp: the people, the conditions. . . . I went around and sketched the conditions, landscapes."

Kango Takamura was a photo retoucher at the RKO Studios in Los Angeles and recorded in watercolor his observations of Santa Fe and Manzanar. "You are not allowed to shoot photographs," he explained. "That's why I sketch exactly what was,

102. Violet Matsuda de Cristoforo, *Poetic Reflections of the Tule Lake Internment Camp, 1944* (Santa Clara: Communicart, 1987), p. ix.
103. Ibid., pp. 30–31.

everything I saw. It was exactly like this." Mine Okubo was creating mosaic murals for the Federal Arts Project in Oakland when she was interned. In Topaz, she said, her friends "on the outside" sent her extra food and "crazy gifts" to cheer her up. "Once I got a box with a whole bunch of worms. . . . So I decided I would do something for them. I started a series of drawings telling them the story of my camp life. At the time I wasn't thinking of a book; I was thinking of an exhibition, but these drawings later became my book *Citizen 13660*. So I just kept a record of everything, objective and humorous, without saying much so they could see it all." Okubo taught art to Topaz's children. "I liked the children and students," she recalled. "It is a two-way learning—we learn from each other."[104]

The vast majority of camp artists were "ordinary" people for whom the creative act, both before and during the war, was a way of coping, of healing, of living. In turn, the act recorded for posterity and conveyed to others the feelings, the thoughts, the experiences of the creators, their times, their places, and their subjects. As artifacts, art from the camps speaks to us today of ingenuity, rare abilities, and imagination, but also of unrelenting persistence, quiet strength, and simple dignity. The ordinary is truly extraordinary. Jo Tominaga recalled happier times before the war. "My father was a workman," he began. "We lived in a neighborhood of out-of-door laborers. He built our little house and made a special garden on our stony plot of ground. When he had completed the garden, he collected all the leftover stones and piled them carefully along the edge of the house, below the eaves. On rainy days, when the neighbors could not work, he would call them in and they would all make poems to the music of the rain falling from the roof to the stones below."[105]

Creativity, we must remember, surged despite the fixity of confinement and the paralysis of rejection. That rejection was underscored when the government rubbed salt in the wound. "The Army recruiting team came into Manzanar around the early part of 1943," remembered Frank Chuman. "We had a big meeting in this mess hall of all persons eligible for military duty with two white soldiers and a person of Japanese ancestry, and this guy was trying to persuade us all to volunteer for the Army, and I'm not too sure whether I got up and spoke back to him or whether I said it in my own mind, but I said, 'Why should we fight for the United States Government as soldiers, when the United States Government distrusts us? Why do they now

104. Gesensway and Roseman, *Beyond Words*, pp. 71, 117, 125, 147, 151, 163.
105. Eaton, *Beauty behind Barbed Wire*, pp. 6, 8.

want us to serve when they consider us to be disloyal? Why do they want us to serve when they have taken us out of our homes and schools and businesses? . . . It doesn't make sense, and so far as I'm concerned I'm not going to do anything . . . until the United States Government does something to remedy this unjust situation.'"

Later that same year, the WRA administered a questionnaire ostensibly designed to determine the "loyalty" of potential military inductees but requiring all Japanese, citizen and noncitizen, women and men, over the age of seventeen to answer the forty questions. Those deemed "loyal," the WRA reasoned, could be drafted into the service but also be issued work and leave permits for resettlement outside the camps. "I was so goddamned mad at that questionnaire," exclaimed Chuman. "It was insulting, impugning without any evidence, just from the top down that there was something that made us Japanese Americans suspect in loyalty, allegiance, that we wouldn't fight for the government and saying now you're going to fight. They don't have to push it down my throat—are you willing to bear arms to defend the United States? That's so goddamned obvious that I would do that that it just really made me angry."[106]

Chuman was not alone. Jack Tono observed that "before the evacuation I was ready to join the Army, because this is the only country that I knew," but after the forced removal and mass detention, "I got educated real fast," he said. Confined by the government at Heart Mountain and asked by that same government to fight to preserve democracy, Tono mused: "You start thinking, where the hell is the democracy we learned in school? Hey, wait a minute now. When I have to give my life up for democracy, I want to see the goddamn thing first. . . . We weren't completely against defending the country," he explained, "but we wanted what we had before first, and then we'd go and fight."[107]

At Heart Mountain, Hawaii-born Kiyoshi Okamoto held "open forums" to discuss racism among the camp administrators, free speech, substandard living conditions, and the injustice of the entire program of detention. His "Fair Play Committee of One" swelled and became the Fair Play Committee, which advocated draft resistance after Secretary of War Henry Stimson announced on January 20, 1944, that the *nisei* would be subject to the draft. The committee's meetings attracted

106. Tateishi, *And Justice for All*, pp. 230–31.
107. Ibid., pp. 169–70.

large and eager audiences, despite the administration's ban on the gatherings, and it was the unanimous sentiment of the 200-member committee, reported Frank Emi, "that drafting nisei from these concentration camps, without restoration of their civil rights and rectification of the tremendous economic losses suffered by them, was not only morally wrong, but legally questionable."

In a bulletin to the camp community, the committee declared: "We . . . are not afraid to go to war—we are not afraid to risk our lives for our country. We would gladly sacrifice our lives to protect and uphold the principles and ideals of our country as set forth in the Constitution and the Bill of Rights, for on its inviolability depends the freedom, liberty, justice, and protection of all people including Japanese-Americans and all other minority groups. But have we been given such freedom, such liberty, such justice, such protection?" the Committee asked. "NO!! Without any hearings, without due process of law as guaranteed by the Constitution and Bill of Rights, without any charges filed against us, without any evidence of wrongdoing on our part, one hundred and ten thousand innocent people were kicked out of their homes, literally uprooted from where they have lived for the greater part of their lives, and herded like dangerous criminals into concentration camps with barb wire fencing and military police guarding it."

The government charged the sixty-three draft resisters and seven members of the Fair Play Committee's executive council with draft evasion and conspiracy to violate the law. During the trial, Jack Tono recalled being held in the county jail—"sixty-three of us were put into a place that only holds twenty-four guys"—and at the end of the first day, the judge, Blake Kennedy, addressed the defendants as "you Jap boys." Hearing that, Tono told his comrades after they had returned to the jail: " 'This son of a bitch, he's got it in for us. Don't have high hopes. This guy, he's going to give it to us.' And sure enough," Tono added, "he did." The judge found them all guilty, sentenced them to three years' imprisonment, and assailed their loyalty: "If they are truly loyal American citizens," he wrote, "they should . . . embrace the opportunity to discharge the duties [of citizenship] by offering themselves in the cause of our National Defense." The seven leaders were likewise found guilty, and sentenced to four years in Leavenworth Federal Penitentiary. After the war, an appeals court overturned these convictions, and on Christmas Eve, 1947, President Harry Truman granted a presidential pardon to all draft resisters, including the *nisei*.[108]

Meanwhile, just as principled, patriotic, and heroic *nisei* volunteered and later were drafted to fight against fascism, but also for the futures of themselves and their families. In the days and weeks following Pearl Harbor, Hawaii's military governor dismissed the 317 Japanese Americans who served in the Territorial Guard, and *nisei* soldiers in the National Guard were disarmed. A soldier described how on December 10, "our rifles, ammo, and bayonets were taken from all us AJAs [Americans of Japanese ancestry] with orders to stay in quarters—not even to go for a 'shi-shi' [urine] break!" Although two days later their rifles were given back to them, Japanese American soldiers in the National Guard were not fully trusted by all of their commanding officers. Those dismissed from the Territorial Guard formed themselves into a volunteer labor battalion that strung barbed wire, completed roads, removed rocks, and built warehouses. The Varsity Victory Volunteers, as they called themselves, "set out to fight a twofold fight for tolerance and justice," in the words of a prominent member.

In May 1942, the military governor recommended that Hawaii's *nisei* soldiers, at the time serving in racially integrated units, be organized into a segregated unit, and in June, 1,432 men of the newly created Provisional Battalion set sail for the mainland. They were hastily assembled and were not told about the army's plans for them. "Before we had any chance to bid goodbye to our loved ones," said Spark M. Matsunaga, "we found ourselves on board a troopship sailing for God-knew-where. Speculation was rife that we were headed for a concentration camp." In Oakland, the men were hustled onto trains that took them to the American interior. A soldier described how on the last day, the train slowed and stopped. Looking across the tracks, the men could see a concentration camp with barbed-wire fences and guard towers. "For half an hour we sat silently in our seats," he said, "thinking only of the worst; many were pensive with grim and hollow faces. Then, suddenly, as if to alleviate our pained thoughts, the train backed slowly out of the yard, switched to another track, and continued on." The men disembarked at Camp McCoy, Wis-

108. Okihiro, *Margins and Mainstreams*, pp. 170–72; and Tateishi, *And Justice for All*, p. 171.

consin, where they trained to defend democracy, and where, in one corner of the base, was the concentration camp that held some of the leaders of their community.

The men of the renamed 100th Infantry Battalion encountered additional indignities. They marched and trained with wooden guns before they were entrusted with real firearms, and some of them were selected for a secret project in Mississippi where on Cat Island they played the enemy for attack dogs trained to sniff the presumed distinctive odor emitted by "Japs." "Most of us were transferred to Cat Island to pollute the island where the dogs were with the smell of 'Jap' blood," recalled Yasuo Takata. "Later results showed that this did not make any difference. . . . Each dog trainer sent his dog out to find us. When the dog spotted us, the trainer would fire a shot and we would drop dead with a piece of meat . . . in front of our necks. The dog would eat the meat and lick our faces. We didn't smell Japanese. We were Americans. Even a dog knew that!" [109]

"I will never go back to the mainland," my father told me. I knew that my father had trained, as a member of the 100th, at Camp McCoy and somewhere in the South, perhaps in Mississippi, but I never fully understood why he disliked the mainland so much. I had gone to college in California and had settled into a teaching position in the Bay Area. I wanted him to come and visit—to see my family, stay at my new home, visit my workplace. I wanted him to feel good about his years of toil, his taking two jobs working day and night to put me through college. Those efforts were not wasted, I wanted him to know, and all that I had acquired was earned through his sacrifice and labor. But for years he stoutly refused to leave Hawaii for a few days in California, until a few months before his death. He made the journey with my mother in tow the winter before his final illness.

I remember it well, that visit. We tried to make it especially comfortable, hoping he would enjoy the mainland and perhaps return again. It could be nice here, we tried to assure him, and showed him San Jose's Japantown and took him to the Japanese garden at San Francisco's Golden Gate Park. One day we drove down the Monterey coast, and his eyes lit up when Fort Ord came into view. He had passed this way, he said, during the war. Only after completing the research for my book Cane Fires did I fully understand my father's opinion about the mainland and his

109. Okihiro, *Cane Fires*, pp. 249–52, 255–56; and Chester Tanaka, *Go for Broke: A Pictorial History of the Japanese American 100th Infantry Battalion and the 442d Regimental Combat Team* (Richmond, Calif.: Go for Broke, Inc., 1982), p. 14.

almost obsessive interest in the war. Having served in the 100th, he often said, was the proudest accomplishment of his life. His army pictures, insignias, unit citations, and his Purple Heart medal were all prominently displayed in our Aiea home. And it was only after I had realized the fate of Hawaii's Japanese during the war that I truly grasped the meaning of his avoidance and fascination.

The "good war," for my dad, was not a matter of masculinity, love of country, or ideology. He didn't set off with the cheers and gratitude of the nation ringing in his ears; he didn't have that comfort. He left Hawaii's shore knowing that his parents were in a little village just outside Hiroshima, that his brother was probably in Japan's military, that his own country distrusted him and his kind, and that his service would likely shield his two younger brothers in Hawaii from internment's sweep. He left behind his newly married bride, who had rushed out to Schofield barracks to spend a few minutes with him, and set sail for the mainland, where White soldiers sometimes taunted the *nisei*, calling them "Japs," where segregation and Jim Crow still ruled the South, where bus seats, benches, and drinking fountains bore the labels "Colored" and "White." My father must have gotten his fill.

So when he stood on Africa's shore facing Italy and the landing that would engage the enemy, my father must have known that the bloody battles ahead would help determine the future of Japanese America. He didn't last very long. Like too many of his comrades, my father was wounded by enemy fire, so severely that he never saw the front again. But those who escaped serious injury pressed on, up the boot of Italy, into France and Germany, where a unit of *nisei* soldiers were apparently among the first Allied troops to open the gates of Dachau death camp in April 1945.

My mother had a premonition of my father's fate. Worried for his safety, she had consulted a Hawaiian *kahuna* (priest) and a Japanese seer. They told her to place cooked rice daily before the family altar in a bowl with a lid to keep it fresh. If the moisture was gone from the lid, they told her, that meant that my father had been killed. My mother performed the ritual religiously each day, forgetting only once and discovering to her horror that the lid was nearly bone dry. Shortly thereafter, much to her relief, she learned that my father had been wounded.

My father must have had his fill of racism, hypocrisy, and sacrifice. He must have known that when President Franklin Roosevelt announced the draft for *nisei* and declared, "Americanism is not, and never was, a matter of race or ancestry," he spoke a lie. And he was likely correct in his calculation that his army enlistment would save his brothers from detention. I discovered that possibility decades later, when in the records of the National Archives in Washington, D.C., I happened across correspondence between a naval intelligence officer and his counterpart at army headquarters in Honolulu. What caught my eye was a reference to Japanese living in the Aiea sugar plantation camp. There among a list of "subversives" recommended for detention was my uncle Shogo, who escaped internment perhaps because of his elder brother's service.

I would like to think that my father's final visit to the mainland was prompted by his realization that his blood sacrifice, and that of his comrades, secured his claim to that land—America—and made possible my education here, my new home, my job. George Aki, a chaplain, described the fighting in Bruyeres, France, in 1944. The men of the 100th and 3rd Battalions, he wrote, "are obedient and brave; they charge right into machine gun fire and are mowed down, but those who can get up, charge again and again in waves, like the waves beating on the shores. Our losses are heavy. . . . My spiritual life is at its lowest ebb," he confessed, "for I see so many of the men, close friends, who are giving their all; too many. The sacrifice is too great." [110] I can understand my father's feeling about the war. The scrolled photographs of his unit that extend across the wall and his carefully framed insignias and medals still hang in the living room of his home, years after his death.

About 25,000 Japanese American men and women served in the U.S. armed forces during World War II: in the 100th, composed mainly of men from Hawaii; the 442nd Regimental Combat Team of *nisei* from the mainland concentration camps; those in the Military Intelligence Service and Office of Strategic Services, who fought in the Pacific war; and women who served in the Women's Army Corps. The 100th and 442nd were among the most decorated, most decimated units of the war, garnering 18,143 individual citations, including a Congressional Medal of Honor and 52 Distinguished Service Crosses, and suffering casualty rates of 680 men killed, 67 missing, and 9,486 receiving Purple Hearts.[111] "If you look at the 442nd boys," said Shig Doi, a veteran, "don't look at their faces, look at their bodies. Then you'll find out how much they've suffered." [112]

110. Girdner and Loftis, *Great Betrayal*, p. 331.
111. Tanaka, *Go for Broke*, pp. 143, 146.
112. Tateishi, *And Justice for All*, p. 161.

"You fought for the free nations of the world . . . you fought not only the enemy, you fought prejudice—and you won," President Harry Truman told the ranks of soldiers of the 100th and 442nd on the White House lawn in 1946. "Keep up that fight . . . continue to win—make this great Republic stand for what the Constitution says it stands for: 'the welfare of all the people, all the time.'" Spark Matsunaga, veteran of the 100th and later U.S. senator from Hawaii, added: "If we the living, the beneficiaries of their sacrifices are truly intent upon showing our gratitude, we must do more than gather together for speechmaking and perfunctory ceremonies. We must undertake to carry on the unfinished work which they so nobly advanced. The fight against prejudice is not confined to the battlefield, alone. It is still here and with us now. So long as a single member of our citizenry is denied the use of public facilities and denied the right to earn a decent living because, and solely because of the color of his skin, we who 'fought against prejudice and won' ought not to sit idly by and tolerate the perpetuation of injustices."[113]

Indeed, the gallantry of the *nisei* soldier failed to complete the "unfinished work" —to open the gates of America's concentration camps or put an end to prejudice. In November 1944, just two weeks after the 100th and the 442nd had rescued a unit of Texans hemmed in by Germans and in the process had suffered casualties that were more than four times the number of men rescued, the Hood River, Oregon, American Legion Post removed the names of sixteen *nisei* from the war memorial commemorating all of the county's residents who served in the armed forces. Among those taken off the roll were Frank Hachiya, who died of wounds about a month after the Legion's action and who received the Silver Star posthumously, and Seiji Nishioka, who lay severely wounded in a Naples, Italy, hospital while his mother, sister, and brother were being confined at Heart Mountain. After resisting a barrage of criticism of its action, including a censure from the American Legion's national office, the Hood River Post finally restored all the Japanese American names, except for one who had been dishonorably discharged, to the plaque in April 1945. Still, a majority of the residents favored "a Hood River without a Jap" and resisted the return of their former neighbors when the Japanese were permitted back to the West Coast after January 1945.[114]

When Wilson Makabe returned to the United States, after having spent over four

113. Tanaka, *Go for Broke*, pp. 167, 170-71.
114. Tamura, *Hood River Issei*, pp. 215-23; and Thelma Chang, *"I Can Never Forget": Men of the 100th/442nd* (Honolulu: Sigi Productions, 1991), pp. 189-90.

months in a hospital recovering from his wounds, he called his brother George in Idaho. "That's when I learned that someone had set fire to our house in Loomis. Apparently it was within hours after the radio announcement that the Japanese people could leave the camps and return to their homes on the West Coast," Makabe recalled. "When he told me that . . . oh, you can't describe the feeling. I remember the pain and the hurt, the suffering in the hospitals in Italy—that was nothing compared to this. I cried for the first time. All that time in the hospital I don't remember shedding a tear, but I cried that night. You wonder if it was worth going through all that." [115]

Hideo Nakamine said that when his younger brother died on the island of Hawaii and "the manager learned I wasn't working on the plantation any more, that I was in the service, he called another younger brother of mine into the office and told him, 'Your family has to move out within 30 days.' That was the only housing my family had," he explained. Nakamine was training in Mississippi, and his family had to move in with his married sister in a crowded house in Hilo and later moved to Honolulu to live with another brother. "My family didn't tell me about this for a long time," remembered Nakamine. "My sister, who used to write to me while I was away, never mentioned to me that the family had been kicked out from the plantation." Albert Oki, a member of the 100th and an attorney with the Veterans Administration, told how the VA discriminated against *nisei* veterans by grossly underrating their physical injuries and thereby cheating them of adequate treatment and rehabilitation. "The rate adjudication department was made up mostly of Mainlanders—white people," said Oki. "Their philosophy was, 'We don't have to help these guys too much. They can survive on poi, rice, fish.' The record of the 100th/442nd didn't mean a darn thing to some of the *haoles*." [116]

But there were also many Whites who continued to fight for justice and an end to prejudice alongside America's Japanese. Estelle Ishigo, daughter of a concert singer and artist, followed her husband, Arthur Shigeharu Ishigo, an aspiring actor, into camp. She has left us her drawings, paintings, and poignant account of a place "wherein wind, sand and snow had swept some minds and souls of all past held dreams, leaving them stark and bare with just enough to cover them and keep them deadly alive." [117] Miles Cary, principal of Honolulu's McKinley High School, super-

115. Tateishi, *And Justice for All*, p. 255.
116. Chang, "*I Can Never Forget*," pp. 191, 192.
117. Ishigo, *Lone Heart Mountain*, p. 86.

vised Poston's schools; Ynez Johnston taught art at Tule Lake; Edythe N. Backus, Kay Damon, and Grace Nichols taught at Poston; and Ruth Fischer taught at Tule Lake. A Heart Mountain internee wrote of a White teacher: "she felt the most constructive thing she could do was to show the Japanese in America that there are some Americans who care and who do not blame the war on them. And so she came way out to this forlorn uninspiring country to add her mite toward maintaining the true American spirit of living."[118]

San Francisco attorney Wayne M. Collins worked on the cases of Fred Korematsu and Gordon Hirabayashi and almost single-handedly sought to disallow the renunciation and "repatriation" of Japanese Americans after the war. Collins, who believed that the mass detention was "the foulest goddam crime the United States has ever committed against a wonderful people," argued from 1945 to 1968 that the 5,766 Japanese who renounced their U.S. citizenship during the war did so under duress and thus their action had no legal validity. "You can no more resign citizenship in time of war than you can resign from the human race," declared an indignant Collins about Public Law 405, which was passed by Congress in July 1944 and allowed individuals to renounce their U.S. citizenship and was seen by some of its supporters as a way to rid America permanently of its Japanese. Collins worked ceaselessly for the renunciants, traveling to Tule Lake, Bismarck, Santa Fe, and Crystal City to counsel them. "I was frightened stiff," recalled Collins, "that if I was not able to be in my office every day early and late that the government might attempt to remove all of them to Japan." Through his efforts, Collins succeeded in having the American citizenship of all but a few hundred of the renunciants restored.[119]

Gradually, Japanese Americans began leaving the camps. Students were admitted into colleges and universities outside the restricted zone, men and women served in the military, and seasonal workers were recruited by employers for field and factory. Others received clearance to "relocate" and start anew. Mine Okubo described her departure from Topaz as having been preceded by "plowing through the red tape, through the madness of packing again," and attending seminars on "How to Make Friends" and "How to Behave in the Outside World," as if Japanese behavior had offended their neighbors and caused their detention. On the day of her departure, she received "a train ticket and $25, plus $3 a day for meals while traveling," and a book-

118. Girdner and Loftis, *Great Betrayal*, pp. 244–45.
119. Ibid., pp. 441–49; Hosokawa, *Nisei*, p. 432; and Daniels, *Concentration Camps*, p. 166.

let, *When You Leave the Relocation Center.* After having passed the sentries, "I looked at the crowd at the gate. Only the very old or very young were left. . . . I swallowed a lump in my throat as I waved good-by to them. I entered the bus. As soon as all the passengers had been accounted for, we were on our way. I relived momentarily the sorrows and the joys of my whole evacuation experience, until the barracks faded away into the distance. My thoughts shifted from the past to the future."[120]

"In just three months Manzanar, one-time 'home' to more than 10,000 people, will be only a memory—a memory of joy and heartache, happiness and fear, of love and hate," wrote Kiyoko Nomura, editor of the *Manzanar Free Press.* "During these three and a half years we have learned the importance of cooperation, patience, and sympathy in order that others not suffer needlessly. We have made lasting friends among people who face the same problems as we do. They will not be easily forgotten." Looking toward the future, Nomura was hopeful: "Our children must know what life is beyond the barbed wire. They have yet to see the bright lights of the city, the traffic signals, streetcars, schools, the corner drugstore, and a million other things that even adults have forgotten. . . . But wherever we go, we must begin again with a renewed faith to build for ourselves and those of our heritage a place of security in this great nation so that our children will never be forced to experience the loss and hardships that we have known these last few years."[121]

Those losses and hardships were made all the more painful by the recognition that the wartime experience was unnecessary and unjustified, and that lives once broken could not be mended again, ever. Who can restore the losses of the Hoshidas and Kuimas, of those who were left behind when families were forced into concentration camps—a daughter who drowned while left unattended and a son who may have died of a broken heart? How did the deaths of James Wakasa and Ichiro Shimoda, both shot by guards at the fence, make America safe for democracy? Emi Somekawa, a nurse at Tule Lake, remembered a pregnant woman who had "a very serious cardiac condition." The baby was born prematurely though healthy, but the mother fell into a coma and was put under an oxygen tent for about ten days. "One day her husband came and said that he just couldn't stand watching her breathing, a very labored type of breathing, day after day," Somekawa recalled. "Would we please take her out of her misery. I was kind of shocked to hear him say that, but I

120. Okubo, *Citizen 13660,* pp. 207–9.
121. Armor and Wright, *Manzanar,* p. 129.

said, 'Well, I will talk to the doctor and see what he says.' The doctor said we had nothing here to offer her, and if that's the wishes of the family, then he'll go along with it. And so then we talked about it and I think it was the next day the husband came back again with his family. This was her fifth pregnancy. He had four children, and they were all still little. . . . They all came. He had made his decision; this was what he was going to do. So he talked to the doctor again, who told me to fix up a fourth of morphine. So I was there. There was a teaspoon there with some water in it, and the father told each child to give the mother a sip of water, and after the last child gave the sip of water, the father did the same thing, and then he was ready for the morphine. That was it. That was it. Right away the oxygen tent was removed and she just went to sleep. You know, I feel this might have been a legitimate thing to do for a woman in that condition," reflected Somekawa. "But I still feel that if we were not in camp, that there might have been some other treatment." [122]

Tom Watanabe's pregnant wife was given pills to take at Manzanar by the hospital doctor. The "medication," Watanabe discovered later, was salt tablets, which caused his wife to bloat severely. When his wife went into labor, Watanabe rushed to the hospital and learned from her that she had twins, both girls. He left her, apparently well, to let her rest and go to his barracks to take a shower before returning. He came back to the hospital to find the doctors "running around," because his wife had begun hemorrhaging. "And so they worked on her and then all I can remember is telling, you know, help me, help me," Watanabe recalled. "Through junior high school in the rough neighborhood and everything like that, I could always protect her physically; but I just stood there holding her hand you know, holding on to her and she just drained away. And after that I don't remember too much, and I don't remember even to this day anyone telling me about the babies. I don't know what happened to the babies. I don't know. That's the part that haunts me. Whether it was carelessness. Or that it was something that was going to happen. I know for a fact that the twins were born and the camp did not have the facilities. I know that." Watanabe was told, after his wife's death, that the twins had both died at birth. He knew that to be a lie because his wife had told him about the twins, and years later he discovered that one of the girls had died on the same day as her mother, but the second girl had lived for twenty-four hours. But at the time, everything seemed to

122. Tateishi, *And Justice for All*, pp. 149–50.

stop moving. "All I know I saw, I saw at the funeral, I saw three caskets. . . . I did not even see the daughters. I didn't see even the birth certificates. I did not even see the death certificates. I don't know what they did with the bodies. Even today I don't. . . . About four or five years ago my sister-in-law in Los Angeles told me that she talked to a friend of hers who said that they knew where the children are buried. But I couldn't find the grave. Been looking and looking and looking."[123]

When my search began, in the early 1970s, through the remains of Manzanar's past, I encountered a silence so deafening that I thought I would explode. Only a few of my generation knew or cared about the injustices of World War II, and even fewer *issei* and *nisei* offered to talk about that dark past. Now in retrospect, I understand that the silence formed a wall around Japanese America, creating a safe space for children to grow up free from the violence and hatred of the world beyond. But the silence was also a harsh lesson learned in the classrooms of the instigators and keepers of the concentration camps. "Be quiet," they told us repeatedly. "Ignore the slurs, scornful gazes, harmful deeds. These are the acts of ignorant people, and they happen only occasionally under unique circumstances of war and crises. Work diligently, don't demand things, and blend in with the majority. Disappear and you will eventually be rewarded. Be quiet, or else." The camps, like all traumas, loomed large upon our collective memory. They told us that we mattered little, we were disposable, we were vulnerable and powerless. Silence bought us peace, they left us alone, but it also required a forgetfulness of the past, an absence of speech and expression, and a negation of identity and self. Silence enveloped and protected the tender shoots but also stunted their full growth and promise.

"At the time, we didn't know what happened," said Ben Takeshita. "I guess he talked about it to my parents, but we were not privy to that." Takeshita recalled how he discovered, years later, his elder brother's ordeal at Tule Lake. Takeshita's brother was a sports teacher in the camp and, despite his avoidance of politics, was seen as a leader of the dissidents by the authority. He was held and questioned for two or three days, Takeshita learned, and "they got to a point where they said, 'Okay, we're going to take you out.' And it was obvious that he was going before a firing squad with MPs ready with rifles. He was asked if he wanted a cigarette; he said no. . . . You want a blindfold? . . . No. They said, 'Stand up here,' and they went as far as

123. Ibid., pp. 95–97.

221

saying, 'Ready, aim, fire,' and pulling the trigger, but the rifles had no bullets. They just went click." When he heard the story, said Takeshita, "I really got mad listening to it, because the torture that he must have gone through. . . . I mean it's like the German camps. Torturing the people for the sake of trying to get them to break down or something."[124]

But people, despite imposed silences, have always cried out against their tormentors, if only in whispers, and new generations (re)discover the intangible past to give them explanations for the palpable present. Silences, too, are freighted with meaning, if we listen. We hear voices everywhere, always persistent, sometimes insistent. They are carried by the wind; they are borne by the dust—the choking dust, the muddy dust, the sterile dust. But it is the dust that is the destination of all flesh and, when the flesh is driven into a maelstrom, can prove irresistible. Michiko Mizumoto pondered the meaning of the concentration camps in her poem "Manzanar."

> Dust storms.
> Sweat days.
> Yellow people,
> Exiles.
> I am the mountain that kisses the sky in the dawning.
> I watched the day when these, your people, came into your heart.
> > Tired.
> > Bewildered.
> > Embittered.
>
> I saw you accept them compassion, impassive but visible.
> Life of a thousand teemed within your bosom.
> Silently you received and bore them.
> > Daily you fed them from your breast,
> > Nightly you soothed them to forgetful slumber,
> Guardian and keeper of the unwanted.
>
> They say your people are wanton
> > Sabateurs.

124. Ibid., p. 247.

Haters of white men.
Spies.
Yet I have seen them go forth to die for their only country,
Help with the defense of their homeland,
America.

I have seen them look with beautiful eyes at nature.
And know the pathos of their tearful laughter,
Choked with enveloping mists of the dust storms,
Pant with the heat of sweat-days; still laughing.
Exiles.

And I say to these you harbor and those on the exterior,
"Scoff if you must, but the dawn is approaching,
When these, who have learned and suffered in silent courage;
Better, wiser, for the unforgettable interlude of detention,
Shall trod on free sod again,
Side by side peacefully with those who sneered at the
Dust Storms.
Sweat days.
Yellow people,
Exiles.[125]

Heart Mountain newspaper columnist Miwako Oana wrote to those "who have never lived within a relocation center, let me say that it is not the end of everything. People are still capable of living and laughing and loving and dying. Cherished friendships are born; unexpected places reveal courage and fortitude,—and faith, to those who have it, shines on."[126] Oana penned those words after having spent two years in America's concentration camps, but that same sentiment—and hope—was expressed at the very beginning of these years of exile. On Terminal Island, as the eviction deadline approached, groups of residents and volunteers toiled frantically throughout the night to pack and load the household goods of those whose lives had changed irrevocably. The electricity had been cut off and the houses were dark,

125. Gesensway and Roseman, *Beyond Words*, pp. 108–9.
126. Eaton, *Beauty behind Barbed Wire*, p. 184.

and because the Japanese were not permitted to use flashlights, they worked in the beam of flashlights held by White friends. Because of the blackout, all was darkness. "But looking upward now and again, one could always pick out the same sure stars in their same sure places, and be strangely reassured," recounted the American Friends Service Committee Bulletin. "Suddenly, out of the darkness, a clear young voice said: 'Well, at least, you can't black out the stars!' "[127]

127. Gesensway and Roseman, *Beyond Words*, p. 142.

Light

Winters in Ithaca can be gloomy, and much too long. The snow piled deep on the ground refuses to melt, and I can but imagine the greenness that awaits the spring beneath the cold whiteness. On days such as these, my thoughts return home, to Hawaii, to the little house in which I spent my childhood. I long to take in the fragrance of the rare mango that grows on the side of the house next to the Nakamuras, to sink my bare feet and wiggle my toes in the red earth of the vegetable garden in the backyard. And no matter how long I've been away, whenever I return, the neighbors always greet me with the words, "Welcome home." Home, this place is always my home.

Tei Endow recalled how when she wrote to the caretaker of her family's property in Hood River, Oregon, that the family had decided to return, "I remember that he replied, 'It's probably best not to come home too soon. Things don't look that good. It might even be dangerous.' We were also warned that another neighbor coveted our farm and wished to buy it cheaply." Hood River's mayor had boasted: "Ninety percent are against the Japs! . . . We must let the Japanese know they're not welcome here." And a news item in the local paper had warned that a "reception committee" would greet any Japanese returning to the valley. Despite their fears, noted Miyoshi Noyori, "when we made up our minds to return, this made me happy because I was going home," and Misuyo Nakamura said that "even though my own birthplace seemed insignificant, I wanted my children to return to their birthplace."[1]

When Wilson Makabe returned home to visit with his friends before being shipped off to the war front as a member of the 442nd, he was shunned by his neighbors who were afraid of being labeled "Jap lovers." Workers at a plant he visited to see a friend held a brief sit-down strike, refusing to work while "the enemy" was on the premises. Makabe had to be placed under "protective custody" by the justice of the peace at the request of the company management until he was picked up by an army jeep. "The attitude of my former neighbors was a great shock to me," Makabe remembered. "I had looked forward to friendly visits with many of them." Instead, his brother reported, Makabe was so angry that he nearly ripped off his soldier's uniform on the spot.

"I had heard of trouble before coming back," recalled Nisuke Mitsumori. "It

1. Tamura, *Hood River Issei*, pp. 224, 225, 226.

227

concerned the question of whether those who had been relocated should be allowed to go back to where they came from," he explained. "People were allowed to leave the camp after January, 1945. They gave us identification cards and told us that the government would give us official permission to return if we brought these identification cards to them. Our photographs and fingerprints were on these cards. It was the government's decision, but we were still called 'Japs' by others. When the first Japanese family went back to Pasadena, the people who received this Japanese family were harassed. Somebody wrote some unpleasant things on their garage door."[2]

The Doi family were the first to return to California from Amache on January 5, 1945. "I found the ranch in much better condition than I expected," said Sumio, the eldest son. "However, there is much work to be done." On the night of January 17, Doi heard the sound of cars on his property and, going out to check, discovered the barn on fire. He and his father managed to put the fire out, and an investigation revealed that gasoline had been sprayed on a wall. Two nights later, Doi heard noises, and when he opened the door shots were fired into the house. Fortunately, no one was hit. When the police arrived, two cars were seen speeding away, and sticks of dynamite with burnt fuses and several used matches were found under a corner of the packing shed.

The Dois refused to move. "They will have to blast me out," Sumio declared. His mother, Masaru, said that they owed it to America to stand up for their rights and shoulder their responsibilities. The Auburn police eventually arrested two brothers who were AWOL from the army, a local bartender and his brother, and three women who had joined the men on the night-riding party. They were out "to have some fun" with people they didn't like, according to the confession of one of the soldiers, and the women testified in detail about the attempts to burn the barn and destroy the packing shed. Those confessions were submitted to the jury along with the testimony of an expert witness who positively identified and linked the dynamite with the defendants. The defense pleaded not guilty, and neither the defendants nor the witnesses on their behalf took the stand. Instead, their attorney described the Bataan death march and charged: "The Japanese infiltrated into this country; we accepted them . . . never dreaming they would stab us in the back." The jury of five men and three women, after a two-hour deliberation with time off for lunch, deliv-

2. Sarasohn, *Issei*, p. 235.

228

ered a verdict of innocence, and a crowd of about one hundred people cheered the freed accused.[3]

"I came back to California in May," recalled Shoichi Fukuda. "Everybody was afraid of being attacked by the white people. The war was still going on at that time, and prejudice and oppression were very severe. The first problem was that I could not find a home to live in. The homes which were formerly occupied by Japanese people were occupied by many black families. . . . I had a very difficult time finding a place to live. When I finally found a house, it was small and dirty. The owner did not honor his agreement, so we had no light. We lived by candlelight for about a month." When Minejiro Shibata returned to his home on Terminal Island, he found no one living there, and "the houses had been broken down and replaced with warehouses for the canning company." He and his wife and children moved to Los Angeles, where they stayed with his cousin until he could find a place for his family.[4]

Riyo Orite described the plight of her daughter, whose husband had left her and their five small children during their internment. Her daughter envied her, said Orite, because all of her children had grown up, and "they didn't cause me any hardships." Rearing five youngsters in the camps as a single mother, lamented her daughter, was a struggle. "We cried together," Orite recalled. "When we finally left the camp, we got up at three or four in the morning and woke up the children. We asked to kindle a fire, then we ate breakfast and got on a train. I couldn't even see where my luggage was. I asked for a flashlight and looked for it. At that time one grandchild was only three months old—just a suckling. It was hard. I pitied the parents with babies. I and my grandchild got on a sleeping car, and the young adults got on a separate coach. We returned to Richmond in the darkness. We went to a special housing area there and were given rooms according to the number of people in each family."[5]

Whites greeted the returning Japanese Americans by passing resolutions favoring their exclusion from town and county, by torching their homes, by refusing to serve them in their businesses, and by smashing their windows. But Whites also formed councils for civic unity that protested against those acts of terror and division and worked for "fair play" for Japanese Americans. Racists drove Wilson Makabe from their work plant, but Whites donated blood so he could live when he returned home from the Italian front after having lost a leg in battle. Whites made

3. Girdner and Loftis, *Great Betrayal*, pp. 388–92.
4. Sarasohn, *Issei*, pp. 236, 237–38.
5. Ibid., p. 236.

threatening phone calls to Japanese American families in the middle of the night and a woman's laundry hanging out to dry was burned, but Whites also greeted the trains carrying the returning exiles, took them to temporary shelters, and helped clean, paint, and repair their homes and gardens.

San Jose's Council for Civic Unity opened the Japanese-language school as a hostel for homeless returnees. Housing, wrote volunteer Gerda Isenberg to a Japanese American still in camp, "is one of the most difficult problems we have to face in relocating people. There are no houses to rent at all." African American and White women surveyed the prewar area of Japantown and discovered that many of the homes were occupied by African and Filipino American tenants who had been attracted to San Jose by work opportunities. White, Black, and Japanese volunteers ran an employment office and the hostels that served as temporary shelters for Japanese Americans from the camps and helped to resettle the tenants who had occupied the empty homes of Japantown during the war. The more than fifty hostels that operated along the West Coast for over a year aiding in the repair of damaged lives were another kind of response by Whites and Blacks to homeward-bound Japanese Americans.[6]

Shizuma Takeshita recalled putting an advertisement in the paper asking for work. "I got a call back from someone saying, 'We don't want you Japs; so go somewhere else,'" he remembered. Takeshita and his wife eventually found work with a White family. "We both did domestic work for them," he explained. "I was almost seventy years old and learned to do chores from my wife. World War II ended while we were working there. We listened to the Emperor of Japan proclaim defeat. We declared our loyalty to the U.S.A., but when we heard that the country of our birth was defeated, we cried." Their son, Takeshita said, had been trapped in Japan by the war and had served in the Japanese army. He thought that he would die, so he sent some of his hair in a letter to his parents. But he survived and rejoined his parents in America after the war with his Japanese wife and their two sons. His daughter-in-law, reported Takeshita proudly, passed her citizenship examination, and "we have six votes in our family now."[7]

Masaji Kusachi was sickened at the sight of his home. "When I returned, I found that my home had been ravaged," he recalled. "All that was left of our furnish-

6. Girdner and Loftis, *Great Betrayal*, pp. 383–410.
7. Sarasohn, *Issei*, pp. 242–44.

ings was the kitchen stove. We had also left many belongings in a locked room, but the locks had been broken. When we opened the door, there was nothing left. . . . Everything was stolen! And the condition of our orchard was deplorable! Our trees resembled willows, because they had not been pruned. . . . If trees are not properly pruned," he explained, "you cannot raise a good crop. But by that time, it was too late in the season to prune, and there were no laborers available during this war time. It was bad enough to discover that our home and orchard were in terrible condition. But when our caretaker presented us with a bill for $1,700, that was a terrible blow! Naturally I was infuriated!" Kusachi threatened to sue the "caretaker," who had profited from "managing" other Japanese American property during the war, and received a check from him for the damages and losses he sustained. "This man had leased several Japanese properties in the valley; he shortchanged practically everyone!" Kusachi declared. "Although he had owned very little money before [the] war, he became a rich man."[8]

"I know some people had a lot of trouble when they returned," said Kane Kozono. "I heard that some found their homes burned down when they came back. . . . Most of my white neighbors in West Sacramento were kind and good to us. A white woman right across the street was a very good neighbor. When we were evacuated, I asked her to keep a strongbox for us. At the bottom of the box were receipts and some papers to prove that my husband loaned money to different people. When I came back here from the camp, she visited me and said, 'Mrs. Kozono, here it is. I brought your box back.' I opened it, and found everything in there just as I put it: the papers, the documents, and all the other valuable things. Nothing was missing." A Chicano family, their former employees, had lived in and taken care of the house during the war, and after their homecoming, the Kozonos housed and employed fellow returning Japanese Americans on the ranch.[9]

But very few of the *issei* could simply pick up the pieces and reassemble their shattered lives. They were too old to begin again. Indeed, many carried on. They rebuilt farms and businesses, cleaned and repainted homes and planted gardens, and joined churches and started a host of organizations to promote the social and cultural life of the community. Many others, nonetheless, found that the war boom had passed them by, that the prewar networks and skills and markets had changed and had been

8. Tamura, *Hood River Issei*, p. 228.
9. Sarasohn, *Issei*, pp. 254–57.

assumed by other hands. They were strangers, once again, in a strange land. A large number of West Coast Japanese Americans remigrated elsewhere during and after the war at the instigation of WRA bureaucrats, who sought to break up the prewar communities through their relocation program, and they established new communities in Denver, Minneapolis, Chicago, and Cleveland. Many returned to the West Coast but resettled in places other than their hometowns. The old communities, like the people's lives, had been utterly changed by the war and the government's social engineers, and the future belonged to the next generation, the *nisei*.

In Hawaii, where the Republican party had dominated the Territorial government since U.S. annexation, *nisei* veterans of the 100th and 442nd helped forge a new coalition of labor, Asians, and Hawaiians that swept the Democratic party into office in the "revolution of 1954." Dan Aoki, one of the leaders of the new Democratic majority, explained that their object was to focus "all of their efforts on breaking down the so-called wall of prejudice against non-whites. As far as the Japanese were concerned, it was very seldom that even when they were trained and educated that they came out on top. . . . We wanted to get Nisei in positions to prove that they can do the job if given the opportunity. They're qualified to do it. All they needed was a chance to do it. That's what we tried to do all the time. . . . We just wanted a non-white person to prove to the people that one doesn't have to be a white person to be a leader." [10]

They proved their point. Masato Doi, Nelson K. Doi, Stanley H. Hara, Daniel K. Inouye, Spark M. Matsunaga, and Sakae Takahashi won seats in the Territorial legislature, and others were elected to local offices. And despite sentiment like that expressed by a U.S. congressman when Hawaii's statehood was being considered, "How can you ask us for statehood for Hawaii when only one-third of the people of Hawaii are Caucasians?" the bill was finally passed in 1959. John A. Burns, then Hawaii's delegate to Congress and the focal point of the Territory's new Democratic party, reportedly responded to his questioner: "Mr. Chairman, I've studied the Constitution of the United States and nowhere does it say that the United States is for Caucasians. I'm not here asking for statehood because of the one-third of the people of Hawaii who are Caucasians, but I'm here asking for statehood because of the two-thirds of the people of Hawaii who are non-Caucasians. My constituents

10. Hazama and Komeiji, *Okage Sama De*, p. 188.

232

may not look like yours, but let me assure you that they are as good Americans, if not better Americans than your constituents."[11] With statehood, Daniel K. Inouye was elected to the U.S. House of Representatives, and in 1962 became the first *nisei* to serve in the U.S. Senate. Spark M. Matsunaga and *nisei* attorney Patsy Takemoto Mink represented Hawaii in the House until 1976, when Matsunaga joined Inouye in the Senate. George R. Ariyoshi became the state's and the nation's first Japanese American governor in 1973.

Comparable forces were at work on the U.S. mainland. Although a small minority, Japanese Americans sought to undo the restrictions of the past and help shape their future by engaging in the political process. A pivotal moment was the passage of the Immigration and Nationality Act of 1952, which removed race as a criterion for naturalization but also introduced a quota system that discriminated against Asian immigration and broadened the grounds for the exclusion and deportation of aliens. But the act, passed during the cold war and over the veto of President Harry Truman, enabled citizenship for the *issei*, the vast majority of whom had been rendered perpetual aliens by U.S. law since 1790. "If they wondered why the rights of their citizen offspring had been abridged in the hysteria of the war, they were too polite to ask and too busy studying for their citizenship examinations to challenge the instructor," wrote Bill Hosokawa of *issei* naturalization. "And in time, tiny old ladies bent by toil, gray-haired old men gnarled by a lifetime of labor, men and women in their sixties and seventies and eighties—usually accompanied by their proud *Nisei* children and even their *Sansei* grandchildren—stood before federal judges and took the oath of allegiance as America's newest citizens. It was a privilege and an honor that had been a long time coming."[12]

On a hot afternoon, I remember standing toward the back of a large room at the elementary school in Waipahu sugar plantation, where my mother had failed to complete all eight grades because she had to work to support the family, watching my grandfather take the oath of citizenship with many others. I recall studying with him, helping him cram for the examination that would ask him about the presidents, the Constitution, the Bill of Rights. Of course I didn't know the irony at the time of a government that had excluded persons like my grandfather from citizenship but that required him to commit to memory and recite the pledge of equality and jus-

11. Ibid., p. 192.
12. Hosokawa, *Nisei*, p. 455.

tice for all. I simply abetted his studies. But I can still remember the glow that came with citizenship, when we piled fragrant plumeria and carnation leis around his neck after the ceremony and stood stiffly as someone took our pictures. His cheeks were red with delight, and he instructed us all to call him "John" henceforth, a real American name, he said.

Another law enacted during the cold war and passed over the veto of President Truman, the Internal Security Act of 1950, held significance for Japanese Americans. Title II of the act authorized the president to apprehend and detain any person of whom there was "reasonable ground to believe that such person probably will engage in, probably will conspire with others to engage in, acts of espionage or of sabotage." The precedents established by the U.S. Supreme Court in its decisions affirming the constitutionality of the World War II Japanese American detention program, proponents argued, provided ample authority for the government's sweeping powers during national emergencies. Between 1952 and 1958, Congress appropriated funds to prepare and administer six sites, including the Tule Lake concentration camp used for Japanese Americans during World War II, in the event of an emergency. Ten years later, during protests against the Vietnam War and rising Black militancy, Edwin E. Willis, chairman of the House Un-American Activities Committee, favored the use of Title II and declared that "black militants have essentially declared war on the United States, and therefore they lose all constitutional rights and should be imprisoned in detention camps."[13] And in 1969, Deputy Attorney General Richard Kleindienst said of student protesters, "If people demonstrated in a manner to interfere with others, they should be rounded up and put in a detention camp."[14]

The Citizens Committee for Constitutional Liberties, formed in 1961 to counter the threat to civil liberties posed by advocates of the "communist conspiracy" of the late 1940s and 1950s, focused upon the Internal Security Act of 1950 as a principal danger to American democracy. Indeed, the 1950 act was a cornerstone of the anticommunist movement's legal base from which to launch missiles against the nation's imagined enemies. The Citizens Committee asked Charles R. Allen, Jr., a journalist who had first exposed the government's six detention camps in 1952, to write a booklet on the subject. It was published in 1966 under the title *Concentration Camps*

13. Frank F. Chuman, *The Bamboo People: The Law and Japanese-Americans* (Del Mar, Calif.: Publishers, Inc., 1976), pp. 327–29.
14. Raymond Okamura, "Background and History of the Repeal Campaign," *Amerasia Journal* 2, no. 2 (1974): 85.

U.S.A. The tract received wide circulation and publicity, and about a month before his death in 1968, Martin Luther King, Jr., joined other African American leaders in expressing concern over Title II and the detention camps.

But it was Japanese Americans who spearheaded the drive to repeal Title II. In June 1968, Raymond Okamura and Mary Anna Takagi began a grass-roots campaign within the Japanese American Citizens League (JACL), a *nisei* patriotic and civic organization begun in 1930, to repeal Title II. According to Okamura, the group believed that Japanese Americans, "as the past victims of American concentration camps, were in the best position to lead a repeal campaign," and "it was imperative for Japanese Americans to assume the leadership in order to promote Third World unity. Japanese Americans had been the passive beneficiaries of the Black civil rights movement," he explained, "and this campaign was the perfect issue by which Japanese Americans could make a contribution to the overall struggle for justice in the United States."[15]

The group convinced the conservative JACL leadership to endorse the campaign, and at its national convention in 1968, the JACL adopted a resolution calling for the repeal of Title II. The effort was joined by Hawaii's *nisei* members of Congress in 1969, when Inouye and Matsunaga introduced repeal bills in the Senate and House respectively. As it turned out, the initiative led by Japanese Americans, "the first group in the United States to have concentration camp experience," according to the *Nation* in a June 9, 1969, editorial, disarmed Title II supporters, who had come to view their opposition as "Negro militants" and "alleged radicals" whose motives might be suspect. In 1971, Congress overwhelmingly approved repeal, and President Richard M. Nixon, on his way to a historic meeting with Japan's emperor Hirohito, stopped in Portland, Oregon, to sign the repeal measure.

Edison Uno, one of the co-chairs of the JACL repeal campaign, reflected upon the meaning of the effort for Japanese Americans. Likening the unconstitutional forced removal and detention of Japanese Americans to rape, Uno wrote: "For over a quarter century the unspeakable crime was quietly internalized by the victims as they suffered in silence from a false sense of guilt and shame and thought of themselves as American citizens unworthy of their birthright. Their unjust imprisonment, which mocked the American tradition that 'one is considered innocent

15. Ibid., pp. 76–77.

235

until proven guilty' created long-lasting psychological problems. The trauma was so great that many believed that they must 'prove' themselves innocent in order to eliminate the preconceived notion that Japanese Americans were categorically disloyal. For the record," he added, "it is well established that not one incident of sabotage or espionage was ever committed by a Japanese American." The repeal campaign that brought together scores of Japanese Americans in a common effort, wrote Uno, indicated a healthy response to the people's trauma, showing that "we realized that we should no longer suffer the pain and agony of false guilt" and instead discovered that "we were truly victims of a conspiracy of officials in government who abused their authority and power in order to victimize helpless citizens." In that way, the campaign to repeal Title II was a coming to terms with the silence imposed by the wartime years and a reminder of the need for constant vigilance in the defense of freedom. "The thrill of victory," foresaw Uno, "must be used to energize the next struggle." [16]

Perhaps what Uno had in mind was his 1970 proposal to JACL for that body to seek legislative reparations for the wartime detention. In fact, others before him, such as James Omura, Joseph Y. Kurihara, and Kiyoshi Okamoto, had argued during the war for governmental redress for the wrongs committed and the losses suffered. But it was Edison Uno who prepared the way for the campaign that would culminate with the passage and signing of the Civil Rights Acts of 1988. Uno contended that monetary payments to the victims of the camps would help to ease their economic hardships and mental anguish, vindicate the loyalty of all Japanese Americans, rebuild their shattered communities, educate the American public about the loss of civil liberties, and ensure that such acts never happen again in the future.[17] Although the JACL passed resolutions supporting redress as early as 1970, very little effort was expended on implementing the project until 1976, when it created the National Committee for Redress, which directed JACL's legislative strategy.

The JACL, however, was not the sole actor in the redress movement. The *sansei*, the third generation, were coming of age; and weaned on the social activism of the 1960s, many were inspired by and participants in the civil rights, free speech, anti-Vietnam War and Third World solidarity, women's, and ethnic studies movements. In 1969, the Organization of Southland Asian American Organizations arranged the

16. Edison Uno, "Therapeutic and Educational Benefits (a Commentary)," *Amerasia Journal* 2, no. 2 (1974): 110–11.
17. William Minoru Hohri, *Repairing America: An Account of the Movement for Japanese-American Redress* (Pullman: Washington State University Press, 1988), pp. 37–38.

first pilgrimage to Manzanar concentration camp, students in northern California organized a counterpart pilgrimage to Tule Lake in the same year, and beginning in 1978 activists held Days of Remembrance in communities and on college campuses to commemorate the February 19, 1942, signing of Executive Order 9066. Several hundred people, of all generations, boarded buses to the campsites, cleaned the graves, and remembered the years of exile. "I came on this pilgrimage out of curiosity, little realizing the impact this trip was to have on me," said Marie Miyashiro. "Many feelings which were repressed, many of my 'mental blocks' were cleansed and washed away as I stood on the ground of our former campsite. Realization that I was here once, that I had lost my father in Tule Lake hit me with such a force. I could not stop my flow of tears. More tears flowed later, but these were all good 'cleansing tears.' I feel good. I'm glad reconciliation has taken place with me."[18]

Another part of that reconciliation was winning vindication from the courts, the very courts that had affirmed the injustice of the mass removal and detention. Peter Irons, a member of the legal studies faculty at the University of Massachusetts at the time, discovered in 1981 that the government's own lawyers arguing the internment cases before the U.S. Supreme Court in 1943 and 1944 complained that their superiors had lied to and suppressed evidence from the court. That finding, Irons told the original litigants, Gordon Hirabayashi, Minoru Yasui, and Fred Korematsu, might make it possible to reopen the cases and clear their criminal convictions. "They did me a great wrong," said Korematsu simply, and so began the effort to right "a great wrong." The team of attorneys pursuing the petitions for a writ of error coram nobis (a rehearing to correct a fundamental error at the original trial) was headed by Irons, Kathryn Bannai, Dale Minami, and Peggy Nagai.

Between 1983 when the first petition was filed and 1988 when the government decided to end the litigation, Fred Korematsu and Gordon Hirabayashi's wartime convictions were vacated, but the judge refused to hear Minoru Yasui's petition, and the government's decision to drop the matter prevented a full hearing by the Supreme Court, which was the only body capable of reversing its decisions. Still, the effort to right a great wrong was a pivotal moment in the unfinished business of the war. "It is now conceded by almost everyone that the internment of Japanese Americans during World War II was simply a tragic mistake for which American society as a whole

18. Tule Lake Committee, *Kinenhi: Reflections on Tule Lake* (San Francisco: Tule Lake Committee, 1980), p. 70.

must accept responsibility," declared Judge Donald S. Voorhees, who heard the Hirabayashi coram nobis petition. "If in the future, this country should find itself in a comparable national emergency, the sacrifices made by Gordon Hirabayashi, Fred Korematsu, and Minoru Yasui may, it is hoped, stay the hand of a government again tempted to imprison a defenseless minority without trial and for no offense." [19]

Meanwhile, the legislative effort for redress continued. In 1976, President Gerald R. Ford, in a symbolic act, repealed Executive Order 9066, and in 1980, largely as a result of a compromise reached by the JACL with the Japanese American members of Congress, a Commission on Wartime Relocation and Internment of Civilians was created by President Jimmy Carter and Congress to ascertain whether an injustice had been committed and to recommend appropriate remedies. The commission was seen by strategists as a necessary intermediate step toward the goal of legislative redress. Groups like the National Council for Japanese American Redress (NCJAR), formed in 1979, and the National Coalition for Redress/Reparations (NCRR), organized in 1980, opposed the commission plan at first, believing that the tactic was simply a way to stall legislative action. NCJAR, led by William Hohri, introduced its own redress bill through Mike Lowry, representative from Washington, but it failed in committee. In 1983, NCJAR filed a class-action lawsuit on behalf of all the victims of the detention camps, and that too eventually failed.

But all of those efforts stirred, then mobilized, a sentiment and movement for redress among a supportive, reluctant, and sometimes antagonistic Japanese American community, some of whom preferred to forget the past. That redress movement, working on different fronts, helped to ensure that the legislative process continued to make progress, and NCRR members lined up and prepared witnesses for the commission's hearings in the summer and fall of 1981, when its nine members solicited testimonies in Washington, D.C., New York City, Chicago, Los Angeles, San Francisco, Seattle, and the Aleutian and Pribilof Islands. Those hearings marked a turning point in the drive for legislative redress by revealing to the government the depth of the people's suffering in the outpouring of their testimonies and by solidifying Japanese American support for the idea of redress. The hearings were a kind of "coming out" for Japanese Americans, who had hidden their shame

19. Peter Irons, ed., *Justice Delayed: The Record of the Japanese American Internment Cases* (Middletown: Wesleyan University Press, 1989), pp. 3–46.

and guilt, unmerited, in the closets of their minds. With their voices, after nearly forty years, they broke the silences of the camps.

"My name is Umeno Fujino and I am eighty-five years old," a witness testified. "It was in January 1942: Seven FBI men arrived in Salinas. One early morning the FBI men showed up at my door and messed up everything in the house. They took a boxful of silk handkerchiefs and scarves. They were probably worth about $200 then. They were just so cruel. They even watched me when I went to the bathroom," she recalled. Fujino was taken to the "rodeo grounds." There she was given a stable that "smelled of horse urine all over and seemed unbearable. I felt as though this was a place for dogs and cats. We suffered so much." Six months later, while in camp, she received a bill for seventy-five dollars. "This was to burn the household goods I left in Salinas," she explained. "I was so shocked and humiliated. . . . Please do not repeat this again and we should be compensated for our physical and psychological losses."[20]

Kanshi Stanley Yamashita told the commissioners that his family was among those evicted from Terminal Island with forty-eight hours' notice. When the eviction order was posted, Yamashita's father had already been picked up by the FBI and sent to the camp at Bismarck, North Dakota. "Without the head of the family, how does a mother, with three children, move out of a house where they have lived for years?" he asked. "Bitter memories of trying to dispose of furniture, a fairly new car, my father's precious sextant and chronometers, and the accumulation of years of living to grubby, calculating and profit-seeking scavengers are still vivid." Yamashita then turned to the charge of the commission: "It is farcical to state that the raison d'être of this Commission is to determine whether a wrong had been committed—rather, its efforts should be directed to rectify the patent wrongs committed against a group, solely on ethnic grounds." After relating some of the skepticism among Japanese Americans about the commission's outcome, Yamashita asked, "What will you members of this Commission do to change the resigned, despairing and fatalistic views of these people who still vividly recall the misery and helpless feelings engendered by the evacuation and have inherited the legacy of bigotry, hatred and racial prejudice?"

20. All of the commission testimonies quoted herein have been taken from *Amerasia Journal* 8, no. 2 (1981): 53-105.

"My name is Alice Tanabe Nehira. I was born 5 June 1943 at the Tule Lake Project in Newell, California," she told the commissioners. Her father, Yoriharu Tanabe, was born in Hiroshima, and despite the mass removal order that left many of his friends "angered and betrayed" and the atomic bombing of his place of birth "where most all of his school friends were annihilated," Tanabe, his daughter testified, was "steadfast in his belief that this nation would someday see the grave injustice of this act [detention of Japanese Americans]." When she was born, Nehira continued, the camp physician performed a tubal ligation on her mother without ever telling her or receiving her consent. She discovered her sterility years later when she was examined for colon cancer. "Today, after thirty-eight years, I am still a victim of prejudice," said Nehira, who told about her discrimination suit pending against her employer. "For over thirty-five years I have been the stereotype Japanese American. I've kept quiet, hoping that in due time we will be justly compensated and recognized for our years of patient effort. By my passive attitude, I can reflect on my past years to conclude that it doesn't pay to remain silent. No one benefits when truth is silent." And turning to the commissioners and their work, Nehira declared: "The final judgment will affect all Americans, now and for all time."

"However painful it is, even after forty years of trying to forget the bitter memories of the indignities and hardships suffered by Japanese Americans as a result of the nightmare of the relocation and four years of incarceration, I dedicate this testimony to my children, Ken, Rei, and Kimi, to my brothers Toki and Dick, and to my late father-in-law Gohei Matsuda, and my former mother-in-law Kama, who lived through the frightening experience of wartime internment, in the hope that the tragedy . . . will never again be endured by any American citizen of whatever race or ancestry," began Violet de Cristoforo. A native-born citizen with a seven-year-old son, a five-year-old daughter, and three months pregnant, de Cristoforo and her family were uprooted and placed behind barbed wire. Her daughter was born "in a horse stable" at Fresno Assembly Center and, on the train to Jerome, developed double pneumonia and remained sickly in Jerome and in Tule Lake, where they were transferred. Her brother Toki was placed in Tule Lake's stockade, a prison within a prison, where "he was repeatedly beaten by the security personnel, so badly that once he was left for dead." Her other brother, Dick, served in the U.S. Army in the

Pacific as a translator and was called "derogatory names" by his comrades and "made to go into caves in search of documents or interrogate Japanese prisoners, always with some Caucasian members of his unit armed with rifles and bayonets at his back because they did not feel he could be trusted." Her father, who lived in Hiroshima, died and her mother was severely burned as a result of the atomic bomb explosion, de Cristoforo discovered after the war. "I . . . hope," she resolved, "that the authorities will give a solemn pledge that they will remain faithful to the provisions of our constitution and that the indignities and emotional stresses we suffered will not be repeated in the future."

The commission recommended, and Congress passed, the Civil Rights Act of 1988, which contained a formal apology from Congress, presidential pardons for those who resisted the eviction and detention orders, recommendations that government agencies restore to Japanese American employees lost status or entitlements because of the wartime actions, and financial redress to Japanese American individuals and communities, $20,000 to each survivor and the creation of a community fund to educate the American public about the experience. In a reversal of his administration's opposition to redress, President Ronald Reagan signed the bill into law on August 10, 1988, bringing to a close another aspect of the camps' unfinished business.

But the totality of that business will only be completed when we can ensure that the violation will "never again be endured by any American citizen," in de Cristoforo's words, and that assurance—that racism (or sexism or homophobia or nativism) will never again shape and justify government policy and action—can only be given when we the people resolve it. Indeed, that promise, to past and future generations, is numbered by the days of our remembrance. My pilgrimage, on reflection, must have been impelled by the silences and whispers all around me. I discovered a great truth that Manzanar spring day, when surrounded by the silences of the snow-flecked mountains, the barren desert sand, and the stone and concrete foundations; I found a quickening in the wasteland, a scent in the wind. The burial ground was overfull with life. The silences of the past, I discovered, were not empty of meaning. Our stories, if missing from the pages of history, advance other stories, other lives. Our pauses define the parameters of words and make sense of speech. Mute photographs convey universes of signification, and cold, lifeless objects emit forever the warmth of the hands that made, used, and inhabited them. Silences speak.

In the summer of 1993, my mother and my family—Sean, Colin, Libby, and me—traveled to Japan. The trip, we planned, would combine sightseeing with introductions to and visits with relatives, including aunts and uncles, cousins and their children. Besides, my mother told us, staying with relatives would make the trip less expensive. We hadn't figured on how profoundly that summer would affect us. For me, the visit brought a sense of completeness, of wholeness that I hadn't gotten from my first visit to Japan over twenty years earlier. Our children too felt this connectedness, almost intuitively. In planning the itinerary, we thought that visits with family would dull the excitement of "Nintendo-land" for our teenaged sons, so we scheduled, between the mandatory temples and castles, a day's shopping at Akihabara, Japan's famed electronics district. Surely, we guessed, lingering among floors upon floors of the latest games and gadgets would be the highlight of our sons' Japanese sojourn. Much to our surprise, without hesitation or prompting, both Colin and Sean said that the most memorable part of our summer was the visit to the Okihiro farmhouse about an hour's drive outside Hiroshima.

We were all a bit anxious when the *shinkansen* (bullet train) pulled up at Hiroshima station. We strained to see from our windows the faces of those who awaited our arrival. We learned later that the welcoming party shared our anxiety, wondering what we looked like, the first-born son of the Okihiro first-born son, his White wife, and their biracial children. My mother recognized the group immediately. We were introduced to my aunt, Kayoko, my father's younger sister; her husband, Shigeo; my two cousins Hidenori and Hideko; and their children. I looked just like my cousin, my aunt exclaimed, and weren't Sean and Colin tall! We were hustled into two waiting vans and were driven off, amid the car and bicycle traffic and uniformed schoolchildren, to the Okihiro farm.

The expansive farmhouse stood at one end of a valley that was dotted with rice fields and homes and ringed with hills covered with dense stands of trees. My aunt Kazuko, Hideko's and Hidenori's mother and the sole occupant of the Okihiro farmhouse, greeted us like long-lost family members as we emerged from the van. Colin quickly found a tiny tree frog that sat calmly on the tip of his index finger. He loved the place immediately. In the living room, we chatted between bites of coffee-flavored jello, and looking up I noticed a photograph that I recognized as a funeral set in California or the American West. The funeral was for my great-uncle, Aunt Kazuko told us, my father's uncle who had gone to America and had died there in a work accident. I hadn't even known of his existence, my great-uncle who had worked the fabled land, but here in a farmhouse in Japan was his indelible imprint upon Japanese America that was only visible from the other shore.

Of course we would like to see the family cemetery, my aunt announced, and before we had a chance to finish our jello and *mochi* (rice cake), she had us marching outside, along a rice field, and up a mountain trail. At a clearing, smooth stones marked the gravesites of several generations of Okihiros. The place had been well tended. This was the Okihiro part of the hill, my aunt explained, as she opened a bundle of incense for all of us to place before each stone. The blue smoke rose toward the sky, and my mother pointed to a trail that branched from the cemetery and led to the forests above. Your father used that trail, she said, to get firewood.

After we returned to the farmhouse, Uncle Shigeo took us to the stream that ran below the farm. Your grandfather fished here as a boy, he told Sean and Colin, and when we spotted two brightly colored *koi* (carp) making a nest along the riverbank, my uncle remarked on how unusual it was to find *koi* in this stream, and I thought about how my father had chosen the name "Isamu" for Colin because he would be like a *koi*, he said, strong and always swimming against the current, upstream. After a sumptuous dinner at a local restaurant, we relaxed in the evening cool. The Okihiro farmhouse seemed itself again, filled with family and their bedding, which was spread out on the floor of every room from wall to wall. Uncle Shigeo went outside to catch fireflies, and I followed to survey the valley that I imagined as mine, embraced by the shimmering points of light that extended far off into the distance. That night, I slept contentedly, in my father's house.

"I am the wife of Albert Kurihara who cannot be here today due to a stroke he suffered last week," Mary Kurihara explained to the presidential commission in 1981. "My husband is now in the hospital, but he still really wanted to testify. Albert has asked me to deliver his testimony." Kurihara was born in Hawaii and was sent to Santa Anita and Poston during the war. "I remember having to stay at the dirty horse stables at Santa Anita," Kurihara wrote. "I remember thinking, 'Am I a human being? Why are we being treated like this?' Santa Anita stunk like hell." From Poston, he was "released" to do "hard seasonal labor" harvesting sugar beets, "work which no one else wanted to do," and even after camp, "I was treated like an enemy by other Americans. They were hostile, and I had a very hard time finding any job. . . . This was the treatment they gave to an American citizen!" he exclaimed. "I think back about my younger brother, Dan, who was in the 442nd Regiment. In combat to defend his American native land, Dan suffered a bullet wound that damaged one-fourth of his head and caused him to lose an eye. I think back about what happened to my cousin, Joe. He was a World War I veteran and very proud to be an American. . . . Joe was never the same after camp. Once a very happy person, Joe became very bitter and very unhappy. . . . Every time I think about Dan or Joe, it makes me so angry. Sometimes I want to tell this government to go to hell. This government can never repay all the people who suffered. But, this should not be an excuse for token apologies. I hope this country will never forget what happened," Kurihara concluded, "and do what it can to make sure that future generations will never forget."

We will never forget as long as the haunting memories of lonely desert gravesites pursue us still. We will never forget as long as the wind blows cold and hot and the dark gives way to light. We will never forget as long as the grass grows green and the splashing raindrops on stone find their way to the sea. For with commemoration, we define ourselves as human, and with the inscriptions of the past, we reconfigure our destiny. And we will never forget, because this story is about us all. It is our biography, as Japanese Americans, as Americans, as one people. And the silences of meaning will be whispered around the campfires of our consciousness, and with the dawning we will stand, stretch, and yawn, and return to our homes to sleep in the warmth of the sun.

Bibliography

Adamic, Louis. *From Many Lands.* New York: Harper & Brothers, 1939.

Armor, John, and Peter Wright. *Manzanar.* New York: Times Books, 1988.

Beechert, Edward D. *Working in Hawaii: A Labor History.* Honolulu: University of Hawaii Press, 1985.

Broom, Leonard, and John I. Kitsuse. *The Managed Casualty: The Japanese-American Family in World War II.* Berkeley and Los Angeles: University of California Press, 1973.

Chang, Thelma. *"I Can Never Forget": Men of the 100th/442nd.* Honolulu: Sigi Productions, 1991.

Christgau, John. *"Enemies": World War II Alien Internment.* Ames: Iowa State University Press, 1985.

Chuman, Frank F. *The Bamboo People: The Law and Japanese-Americans.* Del Mar, Calif.: Publishers, Inc., 1976.

Daniels, Roger. *Concentration Camps: North America, Japanese in the United States and Canada during World War II.* Malabar, Fla.: Robert E. Krieger Publishing, 1981.

de Cristoforo, Violet Matsuda. *Poetic Reflections of the Tule Lake Internment Camp, 1944.* Santa Clara: Communicart, 1987.

Dooner, Pierton W. *Last Days of the Republic.* San Francisco: Alta California Publishing, 1880.

Eaton, Allen H. *Beauty behind Barbed Wire: The Arts of the Japanese in Our War Relocation Camps.* New York: Harper & Brothers, 1952.

Embrey, Sue Kunitomi. *The Lost Years, 1942–1946.* Los Angeles: Moonlight Publications, 1972.

Embrey, Sue Kunitomi, Arthur A. Hansen, and Betty Kulberg Mitson. *Manzanar Martyr: An Interview with Harry Y. Ueno.* Fullerton: California State University Oral History Program, 1986.

Ethnic Studies Oral History Project. *Uchinanchu: A History of Okinawans in Hawaii*. Honolulu: Ethnic Studies Program, University of Hawaii, 1981.

Fox, Stephen. *The Unknown Internment: An Oral History of the Relocation of Italian Americans during World War II*. Boston: Twayne Publishers, 1990.

Fukuda, Yoshiaki. *My Six Years of Internment: An Issei's Struggle for Justice*. San Francisco: Konko Church of San Francisco, 1990.

Gesensway, Deborah, and Mindy Roseman. *Beyond Words: Images from America's Concentration Camps*. Ithaca: Cornell University Press, 1987.

Girdner, Audrie, and Anne Loftis. *The Great Betrayal: The Evacuation of the Japanese-Americans during World War II*. London: Macmillan, 1969.

Grodzins, Morton. *Americans Betrayed: Politics and the Japanese Evacuation*. Chicago: University of Chicago Press, 1949.

Hazama, Dorothy Ochiai, and Jane Okamoto Komeiji. *Okage Sama De: The Japanese in Hawai'i, 1885–1985*. Honolulu: Bess Press, 1986.

Hirano, Kiyo. *Enemy Alien*. San Francisco: JAM Publications, 1983.

Hohri, William Minoru. *Repairing America: An Account of the Movement for Japanese-American Redress*. Pullman: Washington State University Press, 1988.

Hosokawa, Bill. *Nisei: The Quiet Americans*. New York: William Morrow, 1969.

Houston, Jeanne Wakatsuki, and James D. Houston. *Farewell to Manzanar*. Boston: Houghton Mifflin, 1973.

Ichioka, Yuji. "*Ameyuki-san:* Japanese Prostitutes in Nineteenth-Century America." *Amerasia Journal* 4, no. 1 (1977): 1–21.

———. *The Issei: The World of the First Generation Japanese Immigrants, 1885–1924*. New York: Free Press, 1988.

Irons, Peter. *Justice at War: The Story of the Japanese American Internment Cases*. New York: Oxford University Press, 1983.

———, ed. *Justice Delayed: The Record of the Japanese American Internment Cases*. Middletown: Wesleyan University Press, 1989.

Ishigo, Estelle. *Lone Heart Mountain*. Los Angeles: n.p., 1972.

Ito, Kazuo. *Issei: A History of Japanese Immigrants in North America*. Translated by Shinichiro Nakamura and Jean S. Gerard. Seattle: Japanese Community Service, 1973.

Kashima, Tetsuden. "American Mistreatment of Internees during World War II: Enemy Alien Japanese." In *Japanese Americans: From Relocation to Redress*, rev. ed., edited by Roger Daniels, Sandra C. Taylor, and Harry H. L. Kitano. Seattle: University of Washington Press, 1991.

Kawakami, Barbara F. *Japanese Immigrant Clothing in Hawaii, 1885–1941*. Honolulu: University of Hawaii Press, 1993.

Kimura, Yukiko. *Issei: Japanese Immigrants in Hawaii*. Honolulu: University of Hawaii Press, 1988.

Kitagawa, Daisuke. *Issei and Nisei: The Internment Years*. New York: Seabury Press, 1967.

Kumamoto, Bob. "The Search for Spies: American Counterintelligence and the Japanese American Community, 1931-1942." *Amerasia Journal* 6, no. 2 (1979): 45–75.

Lai, Him Mark, Genny Lim, and Judy Yung. *Island: Poetry and History of Chinese Immigrants on Angel Island, 1910–1940*. Seattle: University of Washington Press, 1980.

Leighton, Alexander H. *The Governing of Men*. Princeton: Princeton University Press, 1945.

Lind, Andrew W. *Hawaii's Japanese: An Experiment in Democracy*. Princeton: Princeton University Press, 1946.

Lukes, Timothy J., and Gary Y. Okihiro. *Japanese Legacy: Farming and Community Life in California's Santa Clara Valley*. Cupertino: California History Center, 1985.

McWilliams, Carey. *Prejudice: Japanese-Americans, Symbol of Racial Intolerance*. Boston: Little, Brown, 1944.

Masumoto, David Mas. *Country Voices: The Oral History of a Japanese American Family Farm Community*. Del Rey, Calif.: Inaka Countryside Publications, 1987.

Matsumoto, Toru. *Beyond Prejudice: A Story of the Church and Japanese Americans*. New York: Friendship Press, 1946.

Misawa, Steven, ed. *Beginnings: Japanese Americans in San Jose*. San Jose: Japanese American Community Senior Service, 1981.

Nakano, Jiro, and Kay Nakano. *Poets behind Barbed Wire*. Honolulu: Bamboo Ridge Press, 1983.

Nakano, Mei T. *Japanese American Women: Three Generations, 1890–1990*. Berkeley: Mina Press, 1990.

National Japanese American Student Relocation Council. *From Camp to College: The Story of Japanese American Student Relocation*. Philadelphia: National Japanese American Student Relocation Council, n.d.

Odo, Franklin S. Manuscript collection of unpublished *hole hole bushi*.

Odo, Franklin S., and Harry Minoru Urata. "Hole Hole Bushi: Songs of Hawaii's Japanese Immigrants." *Mana* (Hawaii ed.) 6, no. 1 (1981): 69–75.

Okamura, Raymond. "Background and History of the Repeal Campaign." *Amerasia Journal* 2, no. 2 (1974): 73–94.

Okihiro, Gary Y. *Cane Fires: The Anti-Japanese Movement in Hawaii, 1865–1945*. Philadelphia: Temple University Press, 1991.

———. *Margins and Mainstreams: Asians in American History and Culture*. Seattle: University of Washington Press, 1994.

Okihiro, Gary Y., and Julie Sly. "The Press, Japanese Americans, and the Concentration Camps." *Phylon* 44, no. 1 (1983): 66–83.

Okinawa Club of America, comp. *History of the Okinawans in North America*. Translated by Ben Kobashigawa. Los Angeles: UCLA Asian American Studies Center and the Okinawa Club of America, 1988.

Okubo, Mine. *Citizen 13660*. New York: Columbia University Press, 1946.

Okumura, Takie. *Seventy Years of Divine Blessings*. Honolulu: n.p., 1939.

Sarasohn, Eileen Sunada, ed. *The Issei: Portrait of a Pioneer*. Palo Alto: Pacific Books, 1983.

Tamura, Linda. *The Hood River Issei: An Oral History of Japanese Settlers in Oregon's Hood River Valley*. Urbana: University of Illinois Press, 1993.

Tanaka, Chester. *Go for Broke: A Pictorial History of the Japanese American 100th Infantry Battalion and the 442d Regimental Combat Team*. Richmond, Calif.: Go for Broke, Inc., 1982.

Tateishi, John. *And Justice for All: An Oral History of the Japanese American Detention Camps*. New York: Random House, 1984.

Taylor, Sandra C. *Jewel of the Desert: Japanese American Internment at Topaz.* Berkeley and Los Angeles: University of California Press, 1993.

Thompson, Richard Austin. *The Yellow Peril, 1890–1924.* New York: Arno Press, 1978.

Tule Lake Committee. *Kinenhi: Reflections on Tule Lake.* San Francisco: Tule Lake Committee, 1980.

Uchida, Take. "An Issei Internee's Experiences." In *Japanese Americans: From Relocation to Redress*, rev. ed., edited by Roger Daniels, Sandra C. Taylor, and Harry H. L. Kitano. Seattle: University of Washington Press, 1991.

Uchida, Yoshiko. *Desert Exile: The Uprooting of a Japanese-American Family.* Seattle: University of Washington Press, 1982.

Uno, Edison. "Therapeutic and Educational Benefits (a Commentary)." *Amerasia Journal* 2, no. 2 (1974): 109–11.

Wada, Yori. "Growing up in Central California." *Amerasia Journal* 13, no. 2 (1986–87): 3–20.

Wong, Shawn. *Homebase.* New York: Plume, 1991.

Wu, William F. *The Yellow Peril: Chinese Americans in American Fiction, 1850–1940.* Hamden, Conn.: Archon Books, 1982.